AF477502

FRAGMENTS OF WARNING

by

B H Hamilton

www.bookstandpublishing.com

Published by
Bookstand Publishing
Morgan Hill, CA 95037
3945_2

<u>Disclaimer</u>

This is a work of fiction. The events and characters described herein are imaginary and are not intended to refer to specific places or living persons. The opinions expressed in this manuscript are solely the opinions of the author and do not represent the opinions or thoughts of any other. The author has represented and warranted full ownership and/or legal right to publish all materials in this book.

ISBN 978-1-61863-566-2

Printed in the United States of America

Contents

Contents cont.

Contents cont.

Foreword

In the days of Noah we are entrenched. We once more embrace transgressions and declare them our right. We put on the cloak of freedom to hide under its darkness. This is not just a North American problem, nor an Asian, European, South American, African or Australian problem. Neither is it just an Islamic, Hindu, Christian, Jewish, or Buddhist problem. Each self-segregated group points fingers and lays blame at the feet of all but themselves. The stark fact is that our inequity is a world problem. The iron bonds of slavery we have willingly clamped about our wrists, ankles and necks. In blind narcissism we repeat world history at an alarming pace.

As in times past, God is trying to gain our attention. Horrendous natural disasters have hit all nations. Wars have resulted in the slaughter of tens of millions of world citizens. It is most astounding that when we contact our insurance adjuster our claims are denied. The damage is declared as resulting from an "act of God". These are not acts of God but rather the direct results of our rebellion into debauchery. When the protective hand of God is removed all types of evil flourish. God doesn't remove his hand all at once, but gives us opportunities to repent.

But the multitudes of warnings go unrecognized even when tens of thousands or hundreds of thousands of the dead cry out. And if by some slim chance a voice of one of the ministers of God cries a warning, then we condemn the voice as that of a madman. All of Noah's neighbors knew he was a madman too.

As world citizens we each have an obligation to one another to give aid in time of need, to rejoice in time of triumph, to give comfort in time of sorrow, and to try to correct in time of error. In arrogance we willingly accept the first three offers, but stolidly refuse all attempts of correction. In pride we cling to the anchor chains of our enslavement until we drown at the bottom of the deepest trench in the ocean of immorality.

Lies are whispered with ever increasing frequency until they become accepted as truth. One small slip backward at a time goes unnoticed by those whose eyes only gaze into mirrors of delusion. We see what we desire not that which is truly before our very feet.   We build facades of stone, around the nadir of our falsehoods that we've grown to love, in order to keep out all light that might expose the heinous truth of our endeavors.

The following are given in hopes that you may recognize the darkness into which you try to hide your rebellion and that you may begin to seek the truth of God. A voice of possibility cries from the wilderness in anticipation of small rays of responsibility. Are you brave enough to accept responsibility for your own actions? Or will you cling to the assertion of innocence and point your finger at someone else? The freedom of choice rests solely on your own shoulders. I sincerely hope you choose wisely.

A Brighter Light

The years have been many since birth.

Life has seen much hardship but also much mirth.

The light of a child is bright so we say.

Aged, careworn and old we give a weak light at our dusk of day.

This is what the world would have us be.

But you and I know a much brighter light we give, they cannot see.

The light of years and many things seen are best.

We have labored, worked and toiled with little rest.

The brightness of our light is not measured by glow.

Many things learned fed our light as we worked through life's flow.

Don't let the words of the world draw you down.

You are a light so let your smile shine, don't dim it with a frown.

Remember who you are and where you've been.

Build on those things that through life you've seen.

Experiences past have built your life.

Share what you are and give another's day some spice.

A diamond takes years to reach its brilliant peak.

The brightest of all gems cannot be called weak.

Time is the factor that builds so much fire.

Don't forget; let your smile through your eyes twinkle as sapphire.

Share you light so many may know.

The many, many things you have to show.

So let you light shine, don't keep it hidden.

Many people need the brightness don't wait to be bidden.

Take off the basket at every chance.

The flame can shine with a brilliance enhance.

Shine, shine on your light so free.

Let it call out so others may be.

A Hoot 'n a Hunt

The dogs dance in circles, their excitement catches, my heart races.

The moon is not risen, the cold grips, but no matter, anticipation in faces.

Boots, hats, gloves all accounted, prepared for the cold exhilaration.

Ready the dogs released, off like shots in all directions with pent up anticipation.

Carbide lamps filled, topped off with water, yellow lights waltz among shadows.

The hiss and roar softly smokes clipped to our hardhats we drift through the meadows.

The dogs become silent their search begins out of sight an unspoken arc to sift.

Noses to ground, ears tuned, and tails wagging they know their pleasure, their gift.

Voices low, steps measured, awaiting the first bark of the dogs' recognition.

A slap in the cheek, a welt given, released without measure a keen twig's rendition.

Smells intermingled moss, pine, burning propane gas, musty dampness of a specter.

The mists swirl round the creek as the moon rises dancing through the trees like a jester.

New shadows added, wavering, weaving, bobbing, creeping giants stalking silently.

The first bay is tentative a question the second is firm, a chorus of absolution deliberately.

The race is on as the bays become rolling thunder through the hollers and up the ridges.

On moonbeams howls flow out between the stars, tides of sound earthbound by bridges.

To the swift goes not the race, but to the assiduous goes the accolade.

Silent but for one lone voice a mystery turned, flowing parallel, orphan, isolate.

Stretching exhilarating hearts beat, feet pound, woof-woof recognition of hound.

To each owner a dog's voice is indexed, cataloged, and written in mind's eye, bound.

No doubt, Old Red has struck true the path, trail's scent bonded like glue.

Each heart beat pauses to listen a great owl's hoot awakened out of the blue.

Finally others take up the song far behind Old Blue, the owl other hoot-hoots.

The far chorus turns, dips down, then over another razor backed ridge it flows-

scoots.

Double back off the ridge and into the holler, the songs plaintive notes change to

tree.

We move forward in purpose focused single-minded we are --- free.

A Walk in the Shadows

To walk in the shadows is to dabble. Enticed into pleasures of our desires, we stray. Like sheep from the pastures of safety ever we nibble at sweeter grasses. Following our noses soon to the shadows we've willing transgressed. Nibble and bite led on by enticing tastes' pleasures we seek each day, we take and take. The grass in the shadows looks dark green and sweet. To it we rush to get the first bite err another beats us to it. Enticed into following into the shadows we're led. Confused and wandering deeper into the night we've fled. Sweet words, whispered lies inveigle us into the shadow's dark delights. With reason we treason and rationalize our betrayals. It can't be our fault we're just doing our pleasure. Pleasure is good we whisper to one-another over and over till we no long have fears. No guilt remains for we've driven it out with pain. The shadows bind tighter till pain's pleasures we seek. Lost in blindness we are too prideful to admit we no longer have sight. The shadow grows daily fed by greed. From the light we've now fled into the days of Noah. Gone is the fear of the shadows' dark maw. Embraced the night's calling with haughty looks we disdain the Light's truth. A step from the light we believe we can handle. Masters of our destiny capable of self-deliverance we choose to count on our own will-power. Sufficient we argue for our own fate in pleasures untold we ingratiate the shadow. Just a step under we reason is all we need. Dabble a little into pleasures that are free. Just a walk in the shadows we believe we can handle. Willingly imbedded wrapped in the blanket of night we revel. Light's whispered pleading follows for a short time.

America the Fallen

Fallen from light America sailed into darkness on wicked ships of choices freely made. Fallen from truth America took lies to its bosom and clasped them there in acceptance. Fallen from independence America held forth the hands of the ignorant to be bound in the shackles of the enslaved. Fallen from hope America denied the corrective instruction of God. Fallen from faith America's leaders prostituted their charge with the false gods of the carnal minded. Fallen from love America slipped quietly into the chronicles of history repeated. Fallen from grace American slung its nets of deceit into the murky waters of the world's iniquity and harvested hate's catch. Fallen from the true path of enlightenment America dived willingly into the abyss of the Dark Ages and embraced it. Fallen from the promise of principles hammered out by the founding fathers America pulverized the nation's corner stone. Fallen from the heights of the tower of greatness America's fractured foundation could no longer hold the weight of corruption and crumbled. Fallen, slaughtered by the hand of the hammer wielding elected America is nothing more than a memory of hope.

Anticipation

Anticipation is the child's drooling mouth waiting impatiently at the ice cream counter.

Anticipation is in the man's eye as he waits in an unemployment line.

Anticipations are the things hoped for, awaited with expectation.

Anticipations build slowly at times at others in a wave of crashing against a granite cliff.

Anticipation of things sought pursued like a coin by a miser.

Anticipation to heal, succor, from anywhere is expected to be received from everyone.

Anticipations of times changed for the better, improved found.

Anticipations are building a stairway to success, fulfillment or relief.

Anticipate the very best gifts given.

Anticipate the answer expected, proffered freely.

Anticipations grow as a child's expectant waiting for good reward.

Anticipations fulfilled maybe or not our chosen.

Anticipation of boons and gifts without being earned is perilous.

Anticipation of that which we should not have but covet without regard is applauded.

Anticipate an outcome for our children no rod of correction is applied, ruins corrupts.

Anticipate that which is best, work diligently, mold, meld builds character.

Anticipation is a two edged sword which way will you swing?

Anticipation is our striving toward our hope for things better, faith?

Aqua Blue

The aqua blue expanse is broken briefly by the white lapping waves.

The azure dream endures, binds, and draws us in, Love saves.

The sands migrate slowly undulate across the seas.

The crisp edges of the sails pop then fill with the breeze.

The dark shadow of the deep approaches near, threatening a forgotten terror.

The keel grates sheered on the orange coral compounding gash, grave error.

Wind dies; an unholy calm grips, embracing us in a frightful hug.

Groaning from the depths and haunted eyes wide, twitching as a dying bug.

The groans turn to pops and splintering sounds waft up as harsh mists.

Feet shuffle seeking counsel shaking toward the deep defiant fists.

The waters gurgle at first like the tub drain's emptying expulsion.

Alas, not ours, gurgle turns to roar, sails flutter, boat lurches without propulsion.

No land in sight, no radio response, no hope, no life many knees hit the deck.

Hands clasped, prayers lifted in anguish, supplications flow out of the wreck.

Floundering now, keel to the waves, sides shudder once more.

Prayers fervent, bowed knees atremble, hope is all that clings to the core.

At last the rending ceases as water's roar softens a balance is struck.

Breaths held tightly, not a finger lifted, are we saved by luck?

Questions fraught, boat tips, lists, settles sinking all eyes look above.

No luck here abounds tis the hand of God, and of love.

Ass in the Grass

There's an ass in our grass, Mother can't you see. He's nibbling the few last blades that lived through the drought. Come quick and see Papa, he's grazing by the window. He's been ridden from afar just for you and me. I'm not playing, hurry, come and see. There's an ass in our grass. He's hooves have trodden on palm leaves. There are some stuck there still, come and see. A blanket of royal purple drapes across his shoulders. Hurry, hurry don't delay, come and see. The people still line the street. He's passed this way today. A new colt, never ridden his eyes keep rolling back. He's trampled the last grass blades they're broken and will die. Hurry come and see the ass in our grass. He's been ridden for you and me. Just as the teacher's told us on this day it has come to pass. There's an ass in our grass ridden here by the King. Please believe me, you must come and see. There's shouting in the roadway. The people know the truth. We must go and look. The King has passed us by. Please, please hurry or we'll miss our last goodbye. The ass is leaving too; he is trotting back toward home. You must believe me before its too late. The King has come and gone. He tarries here no more; we've missed our opportunity. The dusty cloud is blowing. It is fading into the night. The people have moved away, down the road toward paradise. The purple blanket is fallen and now in the road's dust it lays. Like broken armor it's crumpled and been trampled in the clay. The King has passed this way. Why won't you understand? We've missed the hand that saves. Down the lane He's ridden this very day. Gone now, ran home is the ass in our grass. Soon too the King will pass this way no more. We've squandered our opportunity with daily concerns and false idols we've played. I can no long see darkness has taken us away.

Blessings

Our blessings are numerous, too many to name.

The rain on the grass, the sun on the daisies we can never be the same.

Showers of blessings the old songs refrain.

Food on the table, shoes on our feet many, many blessings we do obtain.

It rains on the poor; it rains on the rich, showers of life for all.

None left out, only a very thankful few rejoice, rejoice the group so small.

The sun glows warm on the wicked, the righteous, the indifferent on each.

The blessings abound a child's laugh, a dove's coo all within reach.

Too many to count, too many to see, open your eyes attend to thee.

Fresh mown grass, warm sand in my toes, look and look we are so free.

Blessing to the right, blessings to the left, blessings can be found all around.

Deep blue sky, white cotton ball clouds our blessings abound.

The smile of a friend, the thunder of high falls, there are gifts galore.

Time swiftly flows as everyone knows soon life's ending we'll be no more.

We rant, we rave, we complain without ceasing.

Open our eyes we must or we will be dead before the reaping.

Blessings abound, no reason to look so down.

So open your eyes seek yea first and your blessing will be found.

Our days are filled with blessings unseen.

Raindrops in the sunlight, a rainbow glistens in a bright mighty sheen.

Blessings unearned free gifts to all bidden.

The nip of a puppy, the purr of a kitten none are truly hidden.

So clear before our eyes, yet unseen they go by.

We work and work for things to be happy so elusive the harder we try.

So open our eyes before it's too late.

Blessings all round now is the time to stop and appreciate.

Showered with love, blessed from above now is the time to see.

So don't look down, blessings all around, all for you and me.

Blue Skies and Pies

Pie day only comes by once every two or three months or so.

The sky is powder blue, the oven is warmed up, and to the orchards we go.

Anticipation sets little mouths a watering, we wait.

While we pick and gather our work makes the pies even more to appreciate.

Apple today, or maybe peach, or plum our work drags; when will we be done?

We climb and clamor, shake and stammer and toss and roll making it fun.

The apples elude us at times to the ground they bounce.

The barn cats around the tree trunks play waiting for a chance to pounce.

The baskets are overflowing as yellow jackets around us buzz.

We swat and duck hoping not to be stung as one alights and tickles my ear fuzz.

The blue sky smiles at our play not a cloud to be seen.

The cow, bell jangles the next field over she works hard her calf to wean.

Our baskets are now filled; the sled slowly drawn comes to collect.

Old Jacob stands patiently one ear up one down his lip the choicest grass to select.

We struggle two to a basket the weight as much as one of us.

Placed carefully in the sled we pile them on without fuss.

To walk is folly to ride the sled jolly; I balance precariously my toes on the runner.

Quicker to walk Old Jacob plods a snail's usual pace, to ride is much funner.

My mouth waters as the pie lined window approaches.

What will it be today no one knows as we pull up in our imagined coaches?

Blue skies above, green grass between our toes, to the kitchen we run.

Hand cranked ice cream on the table awaits, nose smells peaches how fun.

Borrowed

We sit in the sunlit shafts of yellow daisy light. Our time is borrowed like a pencil. If we don't sharpen it often our lives dull and become ineffectual. We are trapped in the lies of self-deceit stricken in the belief that we own, control, manipulate all that is us, all that surrounds us. Borrowed air not ours, a gift from trees, grass, algae and flowers is imbedded design of God's harmony. A house we call ours built, bought, earned we declare it home, but we lie. We've rented it for only a short time, under lease purposes served. Farmland we toil, sow and reap that which we call our own. We buy, sell, and waste what we say we've deserved. Gifts are not earned, but given on loan as books from the library. The water from the faucet we drink thanking the perceived benefactors the municipalities, the water districts. A free gift from the cycles of God's design, again we lay claim and lie and then die. Only borrowed to quench our thirsts, wash our cars, and water our crops but in the end is returned, recycled into the design. Ancestors harnessed it, lay claim to its heat to dispel the cold's bite, fire makers all. In truth the boon of fire was not made by the hands of men. Borrowed from the lightening strike, the volcano's belch, or friction fire became a debt. We claim to make, to create but we lie; visions' free gift, on loan from a tree, sand, rock, flower, and clay all are leased for a short while. Our bodies are ours, claimed, owned, possessed until death. We steal authority to do what we want. Pierced, tattooed, slashed, aborted, contorted, stricken, starved, displayed, perverted, bloated with life's gluttonous endeavors we claim to have the right. Once again we lie, we die. Living temples of the living God under lease to us for three score and ten, we own nothing. We cannot give life but in arrogance we take it. Everything that we are or have, touch, smell, hear or see is barrowed. We are short termed stewards of God's designs.   We best remember err we die, remember not to lie.

Brisk Day

The morning sunlight filtered by the golden leaves imparts no heat.

The ice crystals dance, with blue flashes among the branches, can't be beat.

The chattering squirrels jump from limb to limb with ease.

They settle quietly, briefly and chisel the soft nutty center to please.

The forest wakes slowly the night's mists' tendrils peeking around the trees.

Birds chirp softly, wind tosses the leaves as gentle waves of the forest seas.

The night creatures' time to rest begins at the break of day.

The squirrels, birds and butterflies at dawn's beckoning come out to play.

The deer find a quiet nest, safe they blend into the brambles.

Great Horned Owl to his hollow tree retires done are his long night's rambles.

The little forest mouse to his nest wanders, no hurry now owl is in slumber.

Slowly the carpenter ant awakens thawed from the night's chill that had his number.

The light of day grows; the frost flees wailing into the shadows cast by the sun's

rays.

The mists grow thinner, still among the trees for little while plays.

The smell of warm leaves rises, the squirrels stop quickly at the hawk's cry.

They sit up and listen still as a mouse to go unnoticed they try.

The chipmunk chirps a sharp warning from forest's thick carpet of leaves fallen.

His warning is taken up and spread by the squirrels' sharp bark'n and call'n.

They scatter, as dandelion parachutes before a child's lips, in a hundred directions.

The hawk's shadow passes; its menace like an army's insurrections.

Nothing stirs below, all has gone quiet, and the mists hold their breath.

The forest pauses even the hawk is silent, his shadow glides a silent death.

The shadow slices; it scythes the mists ere they close once again.

The forest floor comes back to life the rustling and stirring begin.

Broken

Broken by pride gives birth to recognized errors of pale fate and opens a new door through which terrors flee.   Broken by the weight of guilt a new life may be built. Broken by the patience of time a life is wasted when immersed in endeavors of crime. Broken by the light burning away the darkness of the pit, moths of fear flee searching the darkness for a place to sit. Broken by the fractured shellac of lies flaking into the breezes of hope, memory is carried into the skies. Broken by the wings of freedom we tumble from the lofty crags and crash into the rocks of an earthly kingdom. Broken by the tread of the depraved, the icy bridge of hate fails under the weight of sin craved. Broken by the lashes of correction, a new path is opened before the feet of planned assertion. Broken by the offer of intercession available for the asking, the repentant declare their sorrows for past transgression. Broken by the hands of love, evil flees from the fragments of life fluttering lifted toward the light above. Broken by the rod of discipline, lessons of faith are repeated through the eons for the sake of the childish seeking offers grace. Broken by the nails of the Lamb of our transgressions, we find release at last from the chains of Satan's repressions.

Buttercups and Lavender

The yellow eyes wink among the thorns, brightly they glisten in the dew.

Purple grape smells waft through the air tantalize mouthwatering but so few.

Kudzu or grape juice is hard to discern both lavender beauty but taste without a nibble.

Buttercups in the sunlight a yellow carpet laid down, dew drops scatter in a dribble.

The smells of late spring entice and whisper seduction's voice draws from work.

Purple and green blended by God's hand, lavender dreams the fields' skirt.

To fear is folly, to work mundane, come frolic amid the flowers till day's end.

Yellow, blue and green play the melodies, to joy's will we should bend.

Even old stones in the sunlight beckon with warmth stored up.

Lavender and Buttercups down the mountain spread, springs babble ready for a sup.

To sing and play is jolly; to work is folly so answer the yellow trumpet's call.

Purple hearts opened in the warm sun's rays are fragrant on the breezes for all.

The gifts are free but fleeting, can't you see.

Come jump through the Buttercups up to your knee.

Frolic and play throughout the whole day.

Don't tarry there in your drudgery, but step out be free amid the lavender stay.

Skip and laugh don't pout and frown, sing and twirl, don't sulk and glare.

To be joyous is far greater than wealth, lay down your burden and put away care.

Come play as a child you once knew how.

Our dance can only begin with a very deep bow.

Called

Called home to be no more lost in the wilderness of inequity, redeemed from among the wicked he is saved. Called out beyond the stars to dwell in peace and tranquility she is embraced. Called into the bosom of life to dwell safely throughout eternity he is secured. Called into the arms of the Redeemer to be cradled against all harms she is chosen. Called to dance between the stars biding time till the end of the age he is rejoicing. Called to wander the earth to bear witness to the wickedness of the deceived she is tasked. Called down to slumber among the saints martyred to give testimony to the lost he is exalted. Called to bear fruit to the salvation of the answered she gave birth. Called up to stand at the right hand of the Most High He was slaughtered. Called to kneel at the feet of the Pure One she was humbled. Called to open to the knock of the Savior we have been with life gifted. Called to the scrubbing chamber we have by the blood been purified. Called to stand in righteousness by grace we at the throne kneel. Called to give glory with every breath we are the children of the Most High. Called, answered, saved, secured, chosen, and redeemed from our own ignorance and debauchery we are eternally loved.

Cardinal Way

Blood red robed in self-proclaimed snow-white gowns of purity sanctified only by men. Pomp and circumstance dance about on the backs of the true white snowflakes of life. Heavily burdened by riches untold unknowingly broken and poor. Flitter about on the branches of life pecking up the abundance offered up by the homeless gutter sparrows. Mansions and wealth are denied by empty words but greedily taken up with full pleasures of plenty, comfort and the lifestyles of the rich and famous wax gluttonous with self-indulgence. Red robed haughty and proud rewards of life on earth enjoyed. Pampered in pomp and steeped in tradition lost in doctrine, truth is trampled into the quagmire of the deep pit. Perched on a limb high above all others self-proclaimed vicar holder of life and death and forgiveness by demands of repentance by confession desires only the worship of men. Pharisees sagaciously full of pious knowledge and foolish lies lead untold millions into hell's gate. Ever hunger for power and purpose lost among the high walls of their self-deception labyrinth. Where now wanders the truth between the thorns grown across the gate to the lost path of life? Forsaken for wealth, power and fame above all others worshiped earthly gain. Trampled are the innocent children underfoot with unholy lusts hidden by ever expanding lies of self-protection. Armored behind walls of stone, glass and gold whispered incriminations are swallowed by the maw of hate. Where now? Gone are the truly humble of yore lost in Avalon's mists of time only a whisper of truth remains to stir the cold, cold ashes of that which has been forsaken.

Chosen

Chosen before the foundations were laid, He was there in the beginning. Chosen out of love for the created, He volunteered. Chosen to walk among the mortal creation, He loves us all. Chosen to give the true testimony, He is the living Word. Chosen to wield God's power, He was gifted with the Holy Spirit. Chosen to serve, He was baptized in the water. Chosen to feed the multitudes, He taught in the fields. Chosen because of love, He tried to gather His sheep. Chosen to be the atonement for all, He was betrayed. Chosen to be separated, He prayed. Chosen to walk the path of all sinners, He was humiliated. Chosen to be the last, He became the first. Chosen to be hung with the wicked, He forgave. Chosen to be slaughtered in His innocence, He glorified the Father. Chosen to be the last lamb of redemption, He paved the path to glory with His blood. Chosen to sit at the right hand, He is our Intercessor. Chosen to stand till the appointed time, He is our advocate. Chosen to be the Sword of Justice, He will judge all. Chosen to lead the armies of God, He will be triumphant. Chosen to be the greatest conqueror of all ages, He will be King.

Crawdads and Waterdogs

Little boys play among the rocks and splash through the creek.

Little girls bake in the kitchen and quilt in the den.

Duck chasing and mud brick making are a little boy's week.

Dolly's hair braided and chocolate pies cool show where little girls have been.

Sling shots and dead falls are things that must be learned.

So are chicken plucking, cleaning and cutting meat for Sunday's dinner.

Forty years forward or so we tell ourselves things of worth must now be earned.

No joys, no simple things pursued, now an emotionless derelict is the winner.

Oh, to retrieve the days of youth, little boy's toes in the mud they wiggle.

Forty years should not account for so little love and lack of mirth.

Better it is to play, romp and roam filled with joy given out a giggle.

Better it is to teach our children love and giving from birth.

A childhood of carefree bliss is deserved and should be a right.

Yet little adults we try to mold, form and hammer till nothing of childhood remains.

How to return to joys of youth, by giving, sharing, but not by might?

How do we recapture our lost enlightenment soon filled with fathomless pains?

Little boys should be in the creek with a pail of waterdogs and crawdads at play.

Little girls should remember play is where it's at true joy in simplicity.

Crawdads and waterdogs in my bucket I see, for these I once again pray.

Look, listen, wait for a change that may come we must choose implicitly.

Crossed

Crossed between the stars of fate battling to relieve the bonds of hate; Crossed between the knots of time struggling to unravel the maze of a confused mind; Crossed between the edges of the earth searching for the answers since birth; Crossed between the two arms of exclusion holding firm the gates of confusion; Crossed between the rails of fear fleeing away from the train of tears; Crossed between the cities boroughs cringing from the rich man's sorrows; Crossed between ships of passion steaming toward goals of the lowest fashion; Crossed between the legs of inequity slashing with knives trying to shred ambiguity; Crossed between the rocks of ages grinding together hope lost in the pages; Crossed between the rivers of life struggling in the currents of strife; Crossed between the oceans' hues swimming through the haze of ten thousand blues; Crossed between the fallen trees of crime rapping out the basest rhyme; Crossed between the grains of sand drowning in the image of the promised land; Crossed between the carnal pleasures pursuing lusts with all our endeavors; Crossed between the lies of deceit swayed into running swiftly to defeat; Crossed between the ropes of freedom swinging along in darkness of our own kingdom; Crossed between the interstates' span driving through the fog of earthly man; Crossed between the truth of grace fleeing from our Redeemer's face; Crossed between the teeth of death fallen when we take our very last breath; Crossed, crossed, crossed we have chosen to be lost.

Dailey Miracles

Where have all the miracles gone?

Could it be we no longer see?

Hatred, fear, no faith, a world full of wrong,

Our sight is clouded with our own smog, we can't glimpse Thee.

Where are the miracles as in times past?

What has changed? You, me!

Not Thee, unchanged from the beginning, more sure than stones cast.

Then it must be me, uprooted as a tree.

I have chosen not to see gifts freely given!

Abundances abound, blessings far beyond measure,

I work thinking its all from me, alas I'm driven.

If only eyes could be opened, a life full of treasure.

Dailey miracles abound.

If we only open our eyes to truth,

Like a golden star in the sand, You can easily be found.

A child's laugh, and a bird's song are given, so many forsooth.

Where have all the miracles gone? They're here.

Quietly they bring us laughs, and love.

If we only choose to look, You are near.

We must recall everything we have and are is from above.

Where are all the miracles now?

They are here for us to embrace.

A sunrise, a wave's crash and a gull's cry, wow!

Look all around the true light of love is from God's face!

Despair

Despair leads to despite, hate, fear and self-loathing.

Despite hardens, wraps in a cocoon of granite, impenetrable.

Hate gnaws old bones of desired retribution, sparks gloating.

Fear warps; bends to its will erases hope, and builds walls impregnable.

Differences abound, surround; some acceptable none cohesive.

To whom the choice, what right of might bequeaths?

Stolen, taken or assumed power without empathy unrestrictive.

Like authority usurped by honey lies many weapons it unsheathes.

Like peoples insist on like thinking no room for expression.

Enlightenment is seeking ever groaning, clawing change by demand.

Collective, bound and enslaved to similarity of impression.

One word, one lie, one coercion is given as command.

Sworn oaths given to uphold, to lift and democracy to defend.

Self-interest and self-gain dictators are formed not born.

Freedoms are taken by subterfuge and civic pandering to true choices' end.

The greatest nation is crumbled by pen, map and with a lie freedom is torn.

Doused

Immersed in drudgery chosen by greedy ambitions, a journey of futility is embarked upon. Absorbed into the chaos of Id imprisonment, the uncivilized pursue beastly desires. Soaked in the acid of deceit, the foolish cleave to the embrace of the carnally enslaved. Drenched by the deluge of media subversions, the gullible are recruited into the propaganda machine of the Hitler apprentices. Soused in the liquor of debauchery, the carousers wallow in the vomit of discrimination. Saturated with perfumed seductions; the licentious romp with death between sheets of abomination. Inundated with the muddy waters of confusion; the ignorant refuse counsel from the wise. Marinated in the sauce of inveiglement, the putrid steaks of indulgence sicken the reckless. Sopped in the milk of indifference, the blithe ignore the needy. Sodden with the tears of the innocent, the assassins of truth stomp in the blood of martyrs. Doused in the blood of atonement, the guilty are given pardon for all transgressions.

Enlightened to Death

We are become enlightened we're told and the liars have seduced the sheep.

Wickedness we accept as an individual's rights, the wolves in the end will also weep.

The light burns through all darkness no matter how tight we wrap the lies that blind.

The wicked shout their seductions from the rooftops tantalizing every warped mind.

Naked we stand defenseless shoving away the free offer of the armor of the Living Word.

We know what's best; history repeated denied that we'll end the same a moral turd.

Excreted into the wasteland of our own creation and devoid of truth, we refuse to see.

Lost to light and love we revel in the narcissism of self-indulgence, and are too stupid to flee.

The days before Noah we rebuild with the blocks of ignorance delved straight out of Hell.

The fruits of our sins ripen, the key to the gates of our abyss held ready, we've blindly fell.

Truth is damned by the liars as foolish and the sheep eagerly swallow all lies.

Soon brimstone's acrid smoke will rise and carry to the heavens a myriad of horrid cries.

Why do the masses flee the truth, fear God's very best offer? No answers have I.

Offers to fulfill every heart's desires softly spoken are followed willingly, it makes me cry.

Enlightenment according to the masses is achieved when we reach the bottom of the abyss.

The media grows fat in a feeding frenzy of evil portrayed as right, something is amiss.

Noah's neighbors shouted his madness into the wind driven raindrops of their destruction.

Madman, madman voices proclaimed his righteous acts as they reveled in seduction.

Arrogance refutes the truth and eyes are covered with the hands of the liar and we're
lost.
Enlightenment is perverted and so we are become enlightened with darkness at great
cost.

Euphemisms

Offended by a phrase our conversations become bland with watered down euphemisms.

Offended by truth our lies weave euphemisms of deceit ensnaring the weak willed.

Offended by justice our lawgivers evade inclusion with bills filled with euphemisms.

Offended by freedom the US Supreme Court creates nefarious euphemisms of new law.

Offended by the knowledge of wrong the oblivious embrace history's hidden euphemisms.

Offended by the self-thinker the sheep of delusion prance in euphemisms of hopelessness.

Offended by the Constitution the dictators of euphemism opinions force their wills on others.

Offended by fear of inanimate objects the terrorists rout cohesion with smug euphemisms.

Offended by life the death givers hide behind euphemisms of their murderous intents.

Offended by diversity the bigots blow smoke up mirrored euphemisms to hide their culpability.

Offended by democracy despots of intolerance throw out euphemisms of threats to everyone.

Offended by altruism the egocentric's lies are full of euphemisms against the poor.

Offended by faith the pretenders sing songs embedded with euphemisms about the religious.

Offended by hope the inept chide the optimistic with euphemisms of discouragement.

Offended by poverty the greedy lash the needy with barbed euphemisms of blame.

Offended by love the hate filled diverts the words of salvation with euphemisms of perversion.

Extirpated

A flower of altruism, pulled up from the choking weeds of selfishness, has been acquitted.

A shrub of generosity, dug up from the craggy desert of avarice, faults have been omitted.

A vine of life, deracinated from the thorns of hate, has been granted love.

A tree of hope, transplanted from the orchard of fruitlessness, has been reprieved from above.

A sheaf of forgiveness, removed from the thorns of the cruel, has been shown sympathy.

A fragrant herb of patience, moved from the stones of intolerance, has been allotted empathy.

A blade of faith, uprooted from the midst of the faithless, has been placed within truth's reach.

A cattail of instruction, lifted from swamps of ignorance, has been allowed a chance to teach.

A fern of peace, exhumed from the graves of conflict, has been presented with serenity.

A mushroom of innocence, reaped from the forest of malice, has been removed from inequity.

A sprout of justice, pulled up from the heat of condemnation, has been planted for respite.

A Reed of love, extirpated from the cross of penalty, has been raised to give life to the contrite.

Family

Family is a network of love working together for the good of all its members. Family loves unconditionally hugging through pain and faults to reconciliation. Family breaks the rules of blame, retribution, and vengeance. Family gives hope in times of despair. Family binds the claws of hate to keep out of evil's grasp. Family gives freely of time to listen to whispers of pain. Family plays games for children's delight nurturing and sharing love's patience. Family holds hands in a chain of strength binding weak links into the solid anchors of love. Family unclasps an unwilling link freeing it to flee from love's embrace. Family sends out strings of renewal to make available strands of forgiveness if sought. Family sees across differences of culture, politics, and opinions spanning the gulfs of separation. Family is bound not by blood or similarities. Family gives wings to dreams. Family opens the doors of opportunity to the timid. Family embraces the differences that would oft-times rend apart. Family ties the world with ribbons of yellow empathy giving reasons for humanity's redemption. Family the world over if only we open our eyes to truth, acceptance and love given to all.

Ferns 'n Fairies

The magic is for a child's eyes alone hidden from the cynicism of adults.

The green light fairy dust floats in the dreams of the incorruptible, pure ones.

Innocence lost, blinds, binds a hollow loss unrecognized voices harsh full of insults.

The children know love concurs; opens eyes of righteousness to cherish daughters and sons.

At what point fallen, ceased recognition, sightless seeing without reason or delight?

Foolishly we demand reality, imaginations crushed, hopes shredded, dreams riven.

They jump and titter at our foolish demand but with age and whittling we mold their fright.

Every child fights a good fight but parents persist, slowly consume fantasies no quarter given.

Adults see nothing but childhood games to be outgrown, delivered for sanity's sake.

Most every child's eyes are closed by dark reasoning reality choked, dreams razed.

Ferns 'n Fairies delight the senses dreams fly behind stars a child points a path we cannot take.

If only adults' eyes were open love would claim all in a blessed embrace how we'd be amazed.

Gifts of joy abound the children all know to cherish, partake, rejoice in magic's glow.

They strive to make us see joys their eyes alone behold our hands they grasp and lead.

Tree limbs and moss our steps crush down last years leaves are all we see our minds too slow.

Look, little fingers point through the tree trunks and shadows, but there's more they plead.

The more we smile condescending quirks the harder they try, little tears, recognition sets in.

A little child can clearly see our blind limits, the walls we built around our sight ages past.

Ferns 'n Fairies are for little eyes only the wonders we hide from run from through briar 'n fen.

It's okay Daddy, little words console give comfort knowing the blindness prohibits, holds fast.

Final Frontier

Space we're told is the last unexplored realm the final frontier to discover from earth.

Though we've barely splashed the surface of the deep which science says gave us birth.

From carbon, nitrogen of chemicals they tell life erupted from nothing they can't explain how.

Nine hundred years ago science told us mice spontaneously appeared from dirty clothes, wow.

We trust blindly in nothing learned in nine hundred years ignorance is bliss the masses know.

Forward into the Dark Ages we leap with great joy believing lies too lazy to seek truth, whoa.

Backward evolving could it be we return soon to be no more than monkeys in a tree.

Scientists blinded by the ends decided determined before studied so ignorantly deem to be free.

From monkey to unknown mammal we're told the reversion continues till back an age we go.

Time speeds up like a clock in hyper drive the stars flash by millions of years to change if so.

The scientists all buckle us in their bubble of lies the rollercoaster of their theory provides a great ride.

This point our cousins join us again rats and marsupials and such where now human pride?

The meek shall inherit the earth one day soon to be tailless amphibians slithering in muck.

Next to the sea we return like a fish with legs we're told, where's the link, doesn't it suck?

Slithering, squirming a fish we're to be with gills don't you know, what year 265 million BC?

What came before the fish, an amoeba, bacterium, coral who can say not science, ice unfreeze?

Back to the primordial soup we've slithered spot of nitrogen, dab of carbon, a sulfur drop core.

Science's final frontier achieved what better to be than dab of muck on the ocean's floor?

Forgotten

Forgotten are the whispers of truth we learned as children. Forgotten are the lies we've told to cover the pains of mistakes made. Forgotten are the waves of light that illuminated our hidden sins. Forgotten are the hands of hope that reached out to give escape. Forgotten are the tendrils of seduction that captured us in our own webs of deceit. Forgotten are the nets of love given for salvation from our fall. Forgotten are the nails of strife hammered into the innocent to cover the guilt of the self-righteous. Forgotten are the miracles of a life perfectly given. Forgotten are the words of truth spoken to the ears of the deaf for understanding. Forgotten are the accusations of the wicked toward the blameless. Forgotten are the days of waiting for life. Forgotten are the testimonies of the disciples. Forgotten are the truths laid before the formation of the earth. Forgotten are the martyrs crying out for vindication. Forgotten are the wicked slayers of love. Forgotten are the mistakes of the past repeated. Forgotten are the failures in denial. Forgotten are the drops of blood shed for our inequities. Forgotten are the words of hope given to the enslaved. Forgotten are the chances multiplied for amnesty offered. Forgotten is our guilt in lies layered into protective armor. Forgotten we've become lost in iniquity masked in normalcy. Forgotten we're wallowing in the dregs of time past and have become Noah's neighbors.

Foundation

A foundation of plaster is like the sweet lies of the honey-tongued and soon crumbles in the rain. A soft yielding loam is as words of seduction and blows away with the first hot driving pain. The dry clay firmament seems solid at first like a ceramic column planted in its berth. But as the monsoons soak it comes oozing from the earth. Sand is easy to move and to mold, but the loose grains swallow all with time. Volcanic gravel is light and crunches under foot, but poor foundation material soon to ash it crumbles without rhyme. Sweet whispered lies of decadence make for a fallen house. Build your home on solid rock and fear not the mouse. The Cornerstone laid in the tempered soil of life make the only eternally lasting home. Take in the Cornerstone of truth into the depths of your heart and settle it there and nevermore you'll roam.

Fragments

Fragments of time wasted in bickering fall despondently into dust. Shattered seconds are splintered like icicles struck with a sledgehammer. Time fragments found in the crevices between the ancient sand grains on the beach are washed whispers of the jellyfish they give testimony to the fall. Fragments of love misguided lead to the cataracts of lust. Eon's maw has swallowed us all into the inky blackness of our desire. Fragments of life lived out in hastily forgotten memories of sacrifice fall on deaf ears. Fractured by the pursuing of elusive hardly recognized endeavors of futility we flounder. Bits of royal purple cloth float with the dust mites of eternity's glorious concentric worship. Jagged bits of the Dark Age taste like bitter coffee dregs spilled from the pot into our cups of inequity. Gritty fragments of our failures haunt us through our purposeful pursuits of joy. Stardust glitters golden on the fall of time's hammer striking a final blow on the glacier's last bastion. Time fragments have been scattered like daisy petals torn loose before their time by tiny fingers of hope. Riven conclave of laughter applauds the fate of the lost among enticing gem fragments of delusion. A new quilt block of pattern is made ready to be sewn into the fabric of the universe by the ancient hands of Love. Millennia fragments foster the last two thousand years of hope washed onto the shores of life offered to the humble lost. Searched and found wanting fragmented lies whispered among ancient stones' ears seduced trillions. Babel's legacy of ignorance and striving metamorphosed into the desolation of abomination constructed minaret of the deceived. Fragments of hate brewed from the tea leaves of brotherhoods forgotten family ties rend lives into the abyss. Hope in life fragments of blood droplets sprinkled on crimson clothing made snow white. The fragments of life droplets shed for all who choose wisely are the one true answer to death.

Freedom

Freedom to choose your path to tread granted by orchestrated knowledge of life. Freedom to be full of love and empathy for your neighbor accepted or denied by each act. Freedom to walk paths of confusion gates have opened before your feet. Freedom to rebel against Love is laid open in an empty tomb. Freedom to condemn the innocent is accepted by those hungry for power. Freedom to relinquish self-importance is spread by the living Word. Freedom to tread the clay of your heart till it is hardened into stone cold bastions is spread across green pastures. Freedom to spread love is whispered into the void by the shouts of the apostles. Freedom to shout the lies of the perverse into the ears of the innocent is as painful as a thousand lashes of Rome. Freedom to listen to truth or lies given to all to assure choices is accessible to everyone. Freedom to delve into an abyss of hate with the spades of your ambition is taken up by the dead who walk. Freedom to reach out your hand to the needy kneels before you every day. Freedom to lift up those who hurt into the light of love's opportunity is the stair step toward redemption. Freedom to smother the life of the innocent is repeated in crucifixions of our future's hopes. Freedom to embrace wickedness is accepted by the blind seekers of self-indulgence. Freedom is a two edged sword available to all to take up and either cut their own throats or battle the thorns of life unto true joy.

Glimpse

A flash of insight is given at opportune times for those who hope.

A twinkle of understanding is imparted with words of encouragement.

A flicker of knowledge is bestowed upon those who remain faithful.

A sparkle of illumination is reflected toward believers.

A glint of purpose is let out of the curtain for the steadfast.

A flare of truth lights the path of the feet of disciples.

A shimmer of the harvest ripples through the grain fields of the teachers.

A glimmer of reward peeps through the clouds and shines on persistence.

A burst of grace is given to those who open their door to light.

A glistening of gold greets the eyes of the innocuous.

A patina of rest awaits the weary follower of righteousness.

A gleam of succor shines in the house of those who seek Love.

A shine of a ray of guidance glows on the map of the salvaged.

A glimpse of eternity is given to those who accept grace.

Grimmles & Cooties

Little boys have grimmles she says, dirt behind ears between fingers and toes.

He's quite certain little girls have cooties galore on faces now that's how it goes.

Grimmles are plain for all to see smudge on cheeks and brows too.

Cooties are well hidden not plain to see could even be on clothes like yesterdays stew.

Grimmles galore that's what he wore on ears, neck, nose and chin.

Girls are one big ole cootie that's what he said don't no one go trusting he big fat grin.

Little boy grimmles are smeared all round on pant legs and bibs they can always be found.

Cooties are mostly unseen by the eye but that dudn't mean there not all-around.

Cooties are a well known fact all little boys are aware of them from way back.

Grimmles are not well known you see most little girls ignore them and run ignorant of the fact.

Cooties and grimmles are everywhere don't you see you best open your eye.

Grimmles and cooties begin around two or three they slip their way in I think from the sky.

Cooties and grimmles disappear abruptly round twelve or maybe thirteen, varies you see.

Grimmles are easily washed away with a little soap and scrubbing a sparkly new me.

Cooties aren't so easy to dispel, unseen they may linger but not many give a hoot.

Lil boys around fourteen don't care what little girls may have their hearts take over their boot.

The chase begins as the grimmles and cooties end left with the childhood season.

Teen boys 'n girls make it hard to tell the chaser a pretty smile or handsome face the reason.

Grimmles and cooties aren't near bad as some think fleeting they fly with age gone by.

They didn't really disappear we all still have grimmles and cooties but now don't care why.

Groundhog Grease 'N Taters

Groundhog grease was aplenty that yar it flowed from the plump little pigs in a river.

The population exploded before we knowd it they'd grazed on bout everyth'n in the garden.

The ole steel traps made barely a dent in the hoards they flowed in from everwher all aquiver.

Hound dogs and maddocks we catht a few but summer het was on and ground baked toa hardn.

That yar pappy larned us all to make deadfalls figur 4 he called the trigger we catched da rest.

Granny smoked em all and rendered out the fat in four lard pails full they shor was plump.

All summer we worked to get em et off greens to grow mow didn' work tho we done our best.

Long bout August ole Blue our mule went back to work he'dn't like the heat we bet is rump.

Up plowed the greens, beans and sweet taters they wuz all deadern doornails not a peck tget.

We set out fall cabbage and few letle radishes a final crop of six week beans then we quit.

The tater vines all died and we waited till fall let em dry abit pappy said won't be none I bet.

Pappy was acertan taters galore wed hav, ole Blue come out n sodbuster too lot more than abit.

Taters here and taters thar five thous'n pound so far I seed taters in my sleep the whole week.

We sweated 'n finly got done seemed like a million ton Pappy said twas five thousn pound.

We sold em most to the tater bin with a load and tater hole another work loud no time ta seek.

The first cold day granny het up one ole hog and baked a mess a taters I ete a greasy
mound.

Heather

She smiles a special smile,

that I know is only for me.

It lights her face, and dances

merrily in her warm brown eyes.

In three or four running steps and

a leap she is in my arms.

Her hug is tight and warm.

The memory of her arms will remain with me forever.

It is time to part our tears flow freely.

Though we must say goodbye for now

our hearts will always share a special bond.

The love of a child is forever.

Honeycomb & Bullets

The day has dawned quiet, the bullets have ceased for a short time.

The mists rise over the slate grey fields pocked with the bomb holes' rhyme.

The Panzers squat, broken shells, roar of engines silenced, seek a moment's sanity.

Weariness streaked faces from yesterday's rain of hell's fury, look up for amity.

The end may be near hope without hope young eyes hollowed by fearful preservation.

Sharp sounds elicit instantaneous flinches unknown foes round every corner build reservation.

Grateful faces from windows peering as hollowed eyed as the yanks below but avid.

A few brave souls descend, speak kind words, and give thanks and hugs yesterday so vivid.

The front lines, ground troops, cattle fodder many titles they march to innocent's needing.

Orders plain, need for rest briefly granted, the front lines held despite wounds bleeding.

A child ventures out, smiles reward, hunger beckons a ration shared for a day's nourishment.

Marching feet struggle to push through, a small joy, bright star, hopes eternal replacement.

Led by small hands, hardly more than children themselves follow haggard forlorn.

The mists give way to a new day bullets cease flying by ears numb to the sound, peace reborn

Little hands tug down a path much trod hard pack dirt under boots a dull thud with each step.

Measured, weighed, found almost adequate, friends here untold a whole day's respite we prep.

For the morrow may hold another day of hell's fire, bombs, bullets and the smell of dread.

But for today we give thanks for a rest unexpected supping red wine we nibble stale bread.

The small hand lets go as a sheltered field we enter bullet riddled bee hives all around.

I stare as he scoops a hand in, turns and places dripping honeycomb in my hand not a sound.

A broad smile I can't keep down as my teeth sink in the sweet offer my tongue leaps for joy.

War torn French village where words' meanings unknown a true friend I've found small boy.

Hoppy

Hoppy is happy this sunny day of rest.

Night spent in feast with summer's bounty they're blest.

Long tails have hopped through the night long.

Little ears heard the owl's wing rustling in death's song.

Scattered in less than half-a-heart's beat, revelry fled.

To hesitate is to be caught for the Owl's feast torn and bled.

Hoppy is young and quick, his mother taught him well.

He's the first under the log at the Owl shadow's death knell.

The others have fled swiftly night death missed its mark.

Scattered in fear seeds left on leaf platters exposed, stark.

Little legs are thumping in the night summer's heat.

Owl soars with empty talon to a far limb retreat.

Seed orgy paused as heads are counted none lost.

The owl's frustration is joyous occasion without cost.

The break of sunlight burns the last shadows away.

Little bodies jump to the feast leaves sway.

Seeds gathered in to store for the next feast.

Summer's bounty will fatten the smallest, very least.

The mountain jumping mice's party is over.

It's been spoiled by the Owl's wild herding drover.

Imp

Whispered enticements float in the shadows cast by inglorious imposters. Words of deceit suggest acts of immorality to those without armor. Hints of rebellion tickle the ears of those who listen for rationalizations. Allusions of opulence sparkle before the eyes of the misled. Propositions of transgressions bombard the wavering brides of sedition. Offers of surfeit flood the desires of the rapacious with inducement. Deals of subversion are laid on the tables of the treacherous with clauses of duplicity. Pacts of dissension are orchestrated by musicians of cacophony in melodies of discord. Treaties of the impious are signed by the invisible pens of malice. Settlements of decreed divorce are married with betrayal in the darkness. Citations of quoted euphemisms are uttered to placate the immoral sensitivity of bias-transgressors. Extracts of vanilla are sprinkled on the putrid debauchery of the corrupt to hide their stench. Rumors of wrongdoing are attributed to the innocent to subvert the truth into subjugation. Anecdotes of false witnesses are uttered at the trials of the faithful to condemn fidelity. Chronicles of mendacity are recorded in the journals of the con-artists to swindle the uninformed. Records of reproof are filed in the cabinets of the judgmental to incriminate the wrongfully accused. Voices of attrition erode the stones of complacency and the lukewarm are spewed through the cracks. Counsels of imps are broadcast bombarding the bastions of hope with missiles of discouragement. Sneers of demons are cloaked behind the hoards of the blinded.

Interlude

The breath of life passes quietly among the whispering truths. At first dedicated in newly won freedom adhered to strictures of righteous action. Pursued were the fundamental laws from the stone inscribed by our Benefactor's hand. Taken into the bosom and clasped tightly in the hands of the grace-driven peace grew tall. Soon chipped by incessant hammers of life's distractions wickedness fell into the cracks of granite fractured resolve and sprouted. Watered by the tears of the oppressed and fed by the slave's toil the vines of transgression groped through the darkness. Shadowed murmurs were masked by facades of purity and benevolence as the creepers of hate were fed by hypocrites. Chafed thighs of faith were blistered by the relentless buffing lies of the affluent. Revelry sizzled in the frying pan of extravagance until charred hopes were tipped into the fires of correction. Dust choked visages gazed forlornly upward seeking the light brownly dimmed without illumination paths were lost. Answers rained down bombs innumerable fracturing the peace of the illusions of nations. Old wounds were opened by evocations of promises given in contradiction. Ancient realms reborn fulfilled the words spoken before time started over. Fear cultivated the liana of malice till brambles hid the light. Shackles shed by equality's striving rattled on the pavement of optimism and made a dull thud. Freed from all but themselves the lost floundered into the obscurity of self-indulgence and forgot to reciprocate. Aspirations found release onto the leaves of aversion and tumors were embraced. Greed choked the last seedlings of love and grace fell from the tree of humanity. Our interlude arrived unknown to all but the most watchful and we hold our breath. The pause continues to give cause for repentance unrequited searching for a small glimmer of truth shinning between the thick cords of offenses innumerable.

Into

Into the abyss we leap with all joys. Into time we dive with all fearlessness. Into life we are pushed with much pain. Into school we are dragged with many fears. Into the waters of change we stick our toes testing our reluctance. Into the chaos of abandonment we hurtle our love. Into the streets of dust we roll our timidity. Into the night with open eyes of our blindness we evade our need. Into the desert we willingly stroll dumping the waters of our compassion. Into the mountains we climb striving for our idols with fruitless passion. Into the smog of corruption we wade leaving behind our faith. Into the trees we scurry backward evolving, fleeing our hopes. Into the air we fling our answers to spite trying to efface our guilt. Into the streets we wander lost among our own creations ineffectual creativity becomes stifling. Into the cab of costs we willingly place our lives and are hurried toward destinations of failure. Into the plane of entrapment we fly freely to the isle of morbid vacations. Into the arms of the liar we embrace the false gods and pursue despair. Into the gate of hopelessness we step into the paradise of brimstone and perish.

Jackal

The wearying incessant yapping taps tiny hammer blows of sound into the ears of the wise. The hoards of wild dogs nip quickly at the heels of the haughty lions. Running across the plains in waves of joyous undulations the voracious seek the innocent waiting at the cross roads of change. The predator's watchful eyes see afar off the twinkling of pure light through the inky stage curtains of hopelessness. The race is on and the participants hurtle toward the goal posts of safety err the wavering find purpose. The wise speak softly holding out hands of opportunities for fulfillment to the uncertain. The innocent languish in indecision as temptation's claws imbed more deeply drawing power from hesitancy till death is almost certain. The righteous' tears fall in raindrops of woe as all eyes are locked on struggles repeated. One small step forward and the claws will be torn free the pain of parting is but a brief agony of recognition as truth's salve instantly transcends all else. How few find the courage for the first step as the Jackal's whispered tickles seduce the ignorant with tantalizing deceit and the claw's pain escalates beyond all understanding. One small step and the slavery fetters will be broken by truth and redemption. The choice is at the door, open it and live or hold fast to your uncertainty and be pulled down into the jackal's final embrace.

Journey

The jaded white sails cuddled the gentle breezes as expectation held her breath and the passage became mundane. The scurvy producing pantries were void of hope and the hollow eyed religious voyagers languished. The prayers held firm through the still waters and faith's candle kept flickering into the darkness. The rocks of success crashed upon the bows of despondency and the sails of retribution were furled on the shores of an unexpected beginning. The founded place became a new nest for the damaged, desperate eagle of keen insight and she struggled to begin a new family. The tribulations of molten birth withered the fledgling's wingtips and she hurtled toward the abyss of the forgotten. The chastising finger lifted the brokenness from the despair of the damned and a Godly nation was birthed in great pain. The wobbly newborn's feet were swept from underneath her repeatedly by the iniquitous endeavors of whisper winkers seeking power and she stumbled to her knees. False pious infiltrators, by the gallows ropes, hung the innocent with bold disgrace and their blood cries out from the foundation stones. Ravenous women and children drove the unhappy pilgrims to the slaying of hoards of the unwitting treasure stewards and they were blind to the cornstalk shepherds. The tidal wave of consuming locusts frothed across mountains, plains and deserts washing away the topsoil of ancient peoples. The steam engines of greed multiplied like bunny rabbits with razor teeth slashing the grass blades of industry as they shriveled in the furnaces of the proud. The numerous rebukes of the wrongdoers were summarily ignored and the haughty were brought low by the tithed dollar bill. The wars settled into the dusts of ignorance and still the mulish sinners persisted in endeavors becoming the tenacious. The short peace for a moment's held breath settled in a fine layer of ash on the shoulders of the wavering. The fleeting offers of respite were ignored and the foolhardy undertook the final march of indulgence. The two hundred fifty years for complete corruption was a new world record and mankind devoured once again the forbidden fruits held forth in the softly cupped hands of the suave angel of light as satisfaction's unholy light burned from his hungry eyes and seared the souls of the newly damned.

Joy

Joy is in the eye that sees the ear that hears and the mouth that speaks the truth. Joy is a state of mind that settles like a dove on your shoulder. It can't be bought, bartered, or stolen from those who have it. Wealth does not guarantee it nor does self-indulgence provide it. Being a homeless beggar, a poor widow, an abandoned orphan does not rob you of it. The greatest treasure of life is not of this world and no amount of manipulation can capture it. Sing because the unexpected downpour has soaked you to the bone in your new suit. Laugh at the seeming tragedy of your old age and approaching death. True joy in life is being thankful for the new day when you wake each morning. To look behind is folly to look ahead is to worry to live now is to be jolly. A child knows truth far wiser than we; exuberance abounds through him each day. No worry no pain each day is taken as the same. Joy is a gift of eternal youth neither old nor young aged but not old a baby but wiser than the oldest scholar. Contentment is not joy stifled in decadence. But joy is contentment tenfold into truth. Joyous pain reminds us we are alive. A hammer blow to our thumb during a job well done is it a joyous occasion? To dance at pain and rejoice in death is an unnatural state. True joy sees life in all the day's events. To be alive is to know pain and taste the sting of death. To live is to find the joy in each and every day. Knowledge is joy ignorance is not bliss. The learned are not wise only those who have found true joy are cradled in the hammock of freedom's embrace. Today is a precious gift the present of God to all. Accept the gift and feel the joy release your hate and fear into the abyss.

Kentucky Fall

Orange, red, yellow and brown a vibrant color pallet abounds.

Every October the trees come alive in death, only a few places to be found.

The warmth of the sun's rays melts through the mists on a golden carpet.

Sparkly crystals twinkle and steam swirls forming a misty turret.

Lowly golden leaf, there are many uses for thee.

Dog's bed, mulch for the flowers and child's play are for all to see.

Slumber, nap, death for a reason all the trees are quiet this season.

People glare and mutter only work they see, beauty escapes them no reason.

Through a child's eye we must walk the joy and learn to partake.

Red as aunt Tildy's hat, yellow as a banana mat, we need to stop and appreciate.

The children are smarter than we, if only we would listen.

Orange as the Jack-o-lantern with a top hat sparkling as a diamond's glisten.

Our season is much shorter than the mighty tree.

Should we squander it with worry and hate? Consider the colorful shower and be
free.

Rake, rake, rake we have no time to think, no time for fun.

Stop, smell and listen, a moment in time is a precious gift, so feel the warm sun.

A golden whirlwind about us dances, to join in is blissful.

If we stand and stare and do not embrace we are only wishful.

What will the neighbors think? We ask locked in indecision.

A child never considers any weighty matters, no uncertainty just precision.

To twirl is bliss, to jump a joy, so dive-in in ecstasy.

With rake in hand sweat runs down our noses, back aches in agony.

A wall of refusal to recognize our plight is of our own making.

The pleasure is there, the fun awaits free for our taking.

If only we could let go, dive right in, simple joy we'd find.

Other's opinions we consider, it lock hands to the rake, ourselves we bind.

A shower, of color and a shower of laughter, around us floats.

All we must do is let go inhibition and shed our prison of coats.

Kiln

Birthed from formless clay and molded by the hand of Love, we are formed. Delivered from the universe's embrace and placed in a living incubator, we are nurtured. Purposed for three score and ten past and at the final hour time holds its breath and we are born. Unshaped by the potters' hands our form is left open to persuasions yet unknown, we await our destinies. Influenced by those we love development's steps zigzag a maze of hope through the wastelands of an earthly life. Tainted by human frailties we wander in the wilderness of our own cultivations. Taught by the wise, we seek truth between the rolling stones of confusion. Crushed by a wrong turn, we either lay in despondency or get up and limp brokenly back on the path toward righteousness. Sought by the crude hands of the seductress, we surrender to immoral desire and die or flee swiftly toward the safety of truth. Tantalized by the carrots of wealth and ease, we stride into the pit of insatiability and drown in luxury or wrestle with our Id and prevail unto life. Lured by the sweet lies of the mayfly winged bait, we are hooked and suffocate or cautiously we detect the barb and abandon biting the temptation and are given a reprieve. Coaxed with honey coated promises, we rush headlong onto the broad path of transgression and become lost in the crowd of deluded or we recognize the bee sting and stay on the straight and narrow road of correction. Deceived by the kind words of pretend friends, we embrace disobedience and become condemned or wade through the fog of lies to find our own truth and are forgiven. Tempered by the kiln's heat and finesse of the Omniscient's hand, we are become gems of worth and the hotter the fire and longer the processing the higher the quality of the stone.

Knock

Rapping quietly at the door of choice, salvation waits patiently for answer. Tapping softly at the heart of truth, instruction attempts entrance to open minds. Thumping repeatedly on the backs of the wayward succor tries to give aid to the injured. Jolting persistently the Word shocks the surface of locked minds to release the tumblers of hate. Whacking the cane of correction wallops the willful prodigal and steers him toward a path for a homeward return. Lashing the belt of chastisement stripes the buttocks of the obstinate to soften pigheadedness. Beating the rod of reprimand tries to knock out the peccadillo so that virtue may begin to seep into the broken. Knocking long-sufferingly Jesus awaits the invitation so that He may provide intercession for the guilty.

Labor's Bounty

The summer's toil is mostly done.

Red, yellow, gold the apples hang low in the sun.

The pear tree's fragrance wafts along the breeze.

Hard as rocks they hang until the first freeze.

The fodder shocks stand as emblems of the day.

The corn mostly gathered and in the crib hands made it lay.

The potatoes rolled out by the plow are gathered in piles to dry.

Sun-dried mud crumbles to dust and soon they are to the pan to fry.

The summer's end bounty the harvest work winds down.

Not time yet to rest and there is no reason yet to frown.

The fall's work is not yet done and tis not time yet for winter's rest.

Sweet potatoes, tomatoes, peppers galore are gathered in mounds of the best.

Fall labor's bounty, food to gather and prepare for winter's store.

Canning, freezing, drying at last harvest time is no more.

Pantry full, tater-hole packed, the fruit of labor's bounty carries us the winter
through.

We've labored and toiled the spring and summer through, now rest at last, nothing to
rue.

Our work's rewards lay at our feet our many blessings we see.

Happy are we, hot buttered potatoes, corn, biscuits and apple puree.

Wood gathered, split and now stacked in the shed and dried.

A crackling fire, warm to the bone, we sit and rock without pride.

Last Battle

The battle began at the very first.

It will end with the final at the very last.

Many have partaken, lifting the choking dust, causing much thirst.

The battle for the beginning will carry to the end and reflect the past.

Time has marched steadily forward through the Milkyway's turning.

Men believe they manipulate, control and direct delusion is bliss.

The hand of God orchestrates all from nearby the end will be burning.

Science attempts to manipulate, deceive and mislead nothing but drivel and piss.

Ignorance is much easier to swallow than harsh truth of enlightenment.

Mass delusion is easy, sheep move together when strayed from the Shepherd.

Men strive for all their hearts' desires believing the world their entitlement.

A cliff, abyss, pit or mire we move freely giving our throats to the fang of a leopard.

The truth we crush, bury or flee far from in hatred and indifference.

We clasp the lies close to our bosoms to protect them for all we're worth.

Why so blind, why so cold, why so self-engrossed wrapped in a cocoon of self

interest?

If we abandon light and truth and love then soon we must leave this earth.

We speak of wars, take offense in our self-proclaimed righteousness, to what end?

Warmongers from ancient times we have no satisfaction until the blood runs bridle

deep.

God will take every decision, action and intent and to His will every one He will

bend.

As the Word has written it from the first so it will be until we find nothing to do but

weep.

These choices have been our own freely given, freely taken and used for much

immorality.

To turn to light and Love is most desirable; alas our own blindness prevents many.

A few diligently seek the light with passion and compassion to help others refine

quality.

The mass herd ignores the chosen; they trample and ill use them till there aren't any.

Why is the light so hated, the law used to erase those who would serve the

abandoned?

When did we leave reason behind and pursue war to what end?

If only we stop to consider, work collectively, build not destroy none would be

forsaken.

All differences in the world don't matter faith, hope and love with these we can

mend.

Laughter

Laughter came down as a gift to the oppressed. Laughter bursts forth at the slightest nudge. Laughter is a freely given to those who need hope. Laughter is the outward pouring of love's release. Laughter is the hate purging reward of the blessed. Laughter is the benefactor of good tidings of joy. Laughter provides the endorphins of delight. Laughter opens the gates of rejoicing. Laughter shines in facets of rainbow lights twinkling in the crystals of life. Laughter gives warmth to the cold hearts of the cynical. Laughter opens doors for the spreading of love. Laughter binds together the common knots of friendship with the glue of communication. Laughter melds the chemicals of attraction into one. Laughter shares hopes and dreams of the fantasy driven. Laughter swirls between the stars' dance. Laughter tolls the final hour of the bell clapper's concordance in the book of instruction. Laughter peels past words of strife to the very heart of the elucidation. Laughter grows inward to break the core of trepidation. Laughter is as contagious as the dolphin's chirping tango. Laughter gathers across heritages to darn the rifts of ignorance. Laughter weaves hand-made quilts of hope joining our differences into a beautiful tapestry. Laughter gleans the particles of truth from a room full of lies. Laughter seals the wicked's mouths with stitches of infectious bliss. Laughter releases the shackles of slavery to wretchedness and begins the danced of freedom. Laughter, you should let loose today and be free. Laughter, you should embrace today and join the exclusive club of the freed.

Lick Fork Blues

Hewed stone chimneys are the last bones of the house.

They stand a testament to a community long since abandoned leaving not even a mouse.

Ghosts of fifteen families whisper among the stones, voices float along the creek.

The old road rebuilt as if homeward bound little faces round the oak trees no longer peek.

The well stones have crumbled into the water they've been splashed by hands unknowing.

The fields are now overgrown trees' roots delving downward, limbs upward growing.

Where have all the neighbors gone, what lies were whispered snatched them all away?

The hollers no longer echo with a child's laugh, no whoop or crack of ball, we forget to pray.

The old school house stands empty the chalk board has fallen, alphabet letters hang by an edge.

No more little voices sound to recite their lessons learned, silence abounds not even a pledge.

Migrated north the politicians say, gone never looking back, a better life to be found.

But that doesn't hold full account for the chimney's cry out for children unborn.

No work, no play, nothing to do the young people say, the hollowed hills deserted, bare.

A dream an illusion, factory work, dead without conviction now only eyes of dread stare.

Hollow, used up, old, youthful thoughts of return died forgotten chimneys give proof.

A stray rock, mossy, hints a memory, half eaten hand cut nail, but no wall, no floor nor roof.

Gone but not forgotten, family names etched in teetering stone flowers on the road of
death.
Silent they remember brothers of the chimney the mountain winds play a melody of
breath.
A few voices remain, speaking alone among the empty hollers, a lone echo off the
mountain.
A wisp of memory is all that lingers, hopes forsaken, ambitious dreams of a wealthy
fountain.
The chimney stones weep for loss of love, child's laughter, and rich aromas of
supper cooking.
An old wrinkled hand on a shaky cane, overcoat and gumboots with watery eyes
stand looking.

Life's Journey

Our lives begin before birth with the breath of God our journey starts.

The seeds of life become one, embraced in our mother's womb by the love it
imparts.

Our journey's start is steered by love and peace we do not control it.

Youth comes swiftly and we question the guiding hands rebelling in an angry fit.

The captain of our own ship we demand to be, no room left for whole love to be
grown.

We've planted our fields of blame, greed, and power and soon we'll reap what we've
sown.

Time flows by us in a swift ship, we best take it or our journeys will be in a deep rift.

As adults we are blinder than children we force our own paths and throw out God's
gift.

Our ships are not our own, stewards only we remain, too blind to see the truth of our
path.

A journey of life should be a cruise with God as our captain we could avoid his
wrath.

Life's journey would be so simple if we let the Captain sail us to the very best
ports of call.

When we demand to navigate the waters of faithlessness we sail blindly into storms
and fall.

A blissful cruise we'd have if we just released control to the One who knows
journey's end.

We know best of course, blindly we sail our own ships demanding control at every
bend.

On clouds of peace we could sail, if with open eyes we let go our crayon color life's
maps.

With a view of our journey's wanderings and the mired plodding we'd see many
mishaps.

The sparkling blue waters and brisk wind of the straight narrow path are clear to
God's eyes.
We blindly struggle through the muck turning many times to the right or left we miss
the prize.
Life is a journey enjoyed the most if sailed through with the captain at the helm of
the ship.
The sooner we get on board the better life's journey as we take the very best trip.

Lightning Bugs in June

Lightning bugs in June are a child's delight.

They flicker and glow brighter than the full moon's light.

Laughing hands snatch bugs in the dew laden grass blades.

Light pours between little fingers clasped tight in yellow beamed shades.

Puppy's tail is slapping across bare legs flapping, chasing dreams.

Giggles and summersaults over a yard full of children's joyous screams.

Happiness abounds when we are open to see it reflected in a child's eye.

Admonish from the porch shadows or become a child before we die.

The question is simple enough for anyone who wishes to see.

But the answer is elusive, hidden in plain sight the child's laughter holds the key.

Joy is most contagious if we but reach out and embrace it, frolic un-caged.

Money cannot buy it, power cannot force it, and children are wiser than the aged.

The lessons of life become our chains drawing tighter with time.

We bind our own shackles unyielding and choked we can no longer rhyme.

Turn around and look is all we need do to see clearly faithful joy.

Simplicity is lost when we look but do not see, mired either brazen or coy.

With each turn of the clock's hands we burden our children into little adults.

Molded and shaped till all happiness is smothered in expectation of grown-up occults.

Best spend time with a child today, not in chagrin or impatiently tolerant they're in vain.

Open eyes, open heart, attentive play and joy will blossom again and take away all pain.

Long Tooth

Time of life, time of death have all the long toothed ones gone into the dark night? Passed from knowledge of the wise they are forgotten among the stones of the past. Lying waste unto death or truth's fruitful words filled with life. Fangs of death, silent pads, and long legs are swiftly flowing across the grasslands. Hidden in plain sight among the withered brown grass tawny, tanned long toothed predator awaits death. Life's cycle in time is but a passing thought of mist blowing before the thunderstorm. Silent in the roar of challenge breath is held in anticipation. Life hangs by the threads of desire split in the silence of time. Grasped from beyond the grave held by the raven's claw against the crumbling of the stars breathed silent revelry. The last hooray before the coldest embrace at eon's gate leapt through life's noose and ravaged death. Forsaken lies in truths devised, abandoned into ecstasy. Long Tooth's flow across the grass seemingly unceasing laughter at the King's demise in the tomb's silent embrace escaped. The stars flash in harmonious celebration of the fulfillment. Long before time or the foundation of the firmament built the Word stood. Sprinkled between the joyous, scattered from the final age's dawning and hidden between the grass blades of love riven. Long Tooth's time was but a flash pan of powder on the camera stand of creation. Joyous laughter among the dead resounds between the pillars of the lies given. Fantasy's prophet of devil's whispered seductions enticing the willing into the sweet brown grass of death.

Long Winter's Nap

Softly stirring the wind hints sunlight waning the days grow brief.

The shadows bloom earlier, darkness deepens consuming in grief.

The day's warmth diminished, weakened the dim light a final gift.

Sap's life flow grows sluggish, weaker then ceases the final rift.

Leaves supply halted turned off for the season.

The transformation is swift the vibrant colors give new reason.

One last burst summer's energy is released backward flows.

Proteins, sugars, energy are stored waiting spring root no longer grows.

Cold deepens and winds howl ripping and tearing soon naked we stand.

Stolid, firm roots anchored deeply in earth set by God's hand.

Purposes forgotten for a time, a season of slumber is bestowed.

The design meets the needs, upholds, withstands and is hallowed.

Like ancient monoliths giving to natures forces they are blown bowing.

Creaking and murmuring into the dark windy night they are bent but not cowering.

Five hundred winters' blasts withstood and endured in a deep nap.

Formed for purpose, reason and showered with a single minded collective flow of

sap.

Waiting, knowing time is as meaningless as each winter's cold bitter embrace.

Soon to be broken by the breezes of spring the cold warmth shall erase.

Long months to us the time to grudgingly abide and whittle shavings from a stick

Their crumbs pile mounded dissonance under our feet by a flicker's dim light of a

candlewick.

The trees' eon spanning thoughts are ponderous, unfathomable and out of reach.

If we could only hold still long enough to hear their songs I fear they have much to

teach.

Much we could heal if only we could ponder a single purpose four months through.

Without distraction focused single-mindedly the perfect answer we may find true.

Michaela

Her cries at night kept me by her crib.
A gentle hand and reassuring touch
and she is asleep in minutes.
She wakes with a smile and sleep in her eyes.
She beats the window with little fists
yelling doggie doggie.
I make a noise, she turns
and reaches up
"Out, she says.
I lift her up and down to the floor.
Time has passed we meet again.
She says who's that mommy?
So much she will never remember.
I remember for us both.
Love is forever.

Mists of Avalon

Hidden for all to find who chose to look. Between the green leaves the shafts of sun rays point the way. The gate is barred and the way shut against those whose earthly pursuits have corrupted their sight. Thorns and brambles protect the innocent from the ravaging wolves of hate. The mists of Avalon, alas keep hidden the gate to life. The opaque eyes of the lost are easily taken by the hand and enticed into death by the whispers of the deceiver. The blind lead the blind with words of seduction into haughty endeavors. Repeat words among the gullible lost learned by rote swords against the armies of truth, slaughtered through their ignorance. Hidden in plain sight the eyes of love see no veil. The cataract of greed and arrogant pride keep hidden the way to life. Swirling mists of Avalon point out the gates of truth to the lost who turn from the pursuit of bad choices. As a bright red stop sign glaring through the snowfall it is stark against the white and directs the feet of the humble onto the path of righteousness. Seek yea first the way of Love and Avalon's garden will unfold before your feet. The grass will roll up through time in an emerald wave from the sea of life. Open only to the obedient plunged into the crimson bath of forgiveness raised up as righteous by the never ending intercessions of the living Word. There is but one key to the gate of paradise and all that is required is to reach out a willing hand, accept truth and take the gift from the open arms of Love.

Moonlit Tonic

Copper caldron sits under the full moon's light a hundred facets all aglow.

Its newly hammered surface sparkles in the freshly fallen snow.

Alone it sits beside no other, waiting, the quiet rustling bears witness.

Soon calloused hands will deliver a top like no other, mirrored tail of coil, perfect fitness.

Sour mash added, steady fire kindled, the caldron is blackened under the moonlight.

Clear liquid soon thereafter begins to drip falling diamonds of tonic in the snow white.

Caught in a canning jar's crystal clear prison waiting its brothers to gather near.

A hundred quart jars lined up in a row gently set on a rock shelf calloused hands no fear.

Take one down a sample to test Moonlit Tonic must always be the very best.

Master distiller, lawless man's two gentle calloused hands have no time for idle rest.

Swish and spit get past the burn to flavor and vim in a balanced blend.

First batch from a new kettle is not for sale but makes a fine gift for a good friend.

The peak of flavor is matched by none the third batch it's ready for any fling.

Moonlit Tonic has been made just right the very perfect batch is in time for spring.

Runs are now honed to the perfect pitch flavor flows out in a steady drip.

Tonic in spring makes the heart sing songs of love at weddings by each sip.

Moss

The old hoary oak stood sentinel for three thousand years with a watchful sigh.

Locked, roots delved deep grasping the earth in a desperate grip against the lie.

Stolid, firm, unmoved through the ages it stands witness to the beginning of the end.

Ageless sun, and seasons' rain give time most meaningless as wind's howl to life's bend.

Droughts and famines pass by the way as the sands carried through a flood.

Testament to truth, knowledge held of the first Word of life, gift held out, shed blood.

Moss grown weary and stooped with the burden of time not shaken, faith rooted deep.

The end of the end announced time withheld soon the scythe to thrust in, souls to reap.

Decay of era grasps with a frantic claw lies to seduce, pull sway, strewn leaves litter.

Diamonds sparkle on twigs curled toward the sky, barren, asleep, light cast a-glitter.

Patience, long suffering and life offered daily to all would listen, free one must just accept.

Moss clings in a desperate hug, encircles pleading for love abandoned men's souls' precept.

Gifts abound for those with eyes to see not blinded by pursuit of fate flitting on a lark.

Sentinel, witness, promise of life love and hope given too not just ancient moss covered bark.

Open our ears to hear whispered songs of praise the stars sing, the oak heralds the advent.

Moss blankets the still hearts' waiting breath held against the hopes, boughs no limit extent.

The omen of life from before time, Word of truth held firm the appointment of our
death.
Paid that which we could not, would not, moss covered hoary old oak, where now
our breath?

Necropolis

Fallen away from life, we are oft deposited with great pomp into the necropolis of faded stone metaphors. Laid to rest, though no evidence exists to support the hopeless assertions of the living a brief sleep ensues. Abandoned as a bag of trash carefully placed at the curb of futility remembered by befuddled minds, we await. Hauled in the casket of the compactor truck and ceremoniously covered over by the black smoke belching demon of last rights, we lay incapacitated for a time. The Lilly white garbage bags adorn our rest and the crimson roses of discarded beef tips embrace our last collapse. Tinkling, the bells of contamination ooze dripping from the fringes of canceled life to reawakened murder by treasonous avariciousness. Fallen from death at the hands of the nefarious we are consumed by life. Sprouted from the decay of composted repasts we blossom into bouquets of red and yellow geraniums. Briefly wafting fragrances of subtle ambrosia mixed with hints of putrefaction tantalize hopes of regeneration. Burned the fields of hope wither under the roasting flames of unrepentant transgression as we deny life. Settled into the crevasses of despair ashes of reminiscence pile up into crags of anguishes chosen in life. Hidden under the mounds of upheaval we cower in the armor of lies layered by time and acceptance. Quieted by the weight of an eon's brief flashing we reason to ourselves the guiltlessness of our immoral embraces. Gathered into closets of secreted hoards, we cherish the plethora of desires fulfilled. Held tightly in the embrace of ruin the night passes and a Day of Judgment dawns quickly. Bowed on knees without volition our breath is frozen awaiting a just sentencing.

Nimbus

The radiance grows faint as the light bearers hide their faces. The circle of light has been shadowed by the wicked one's manipulations. The corona's glow from Christian hearts has been dimmed by their imprisonment in the dungeons of the religiously fractured. The aura of love has been broken by the clubs of sinful self-seekers. The luminosity of the angels has been shrouded by pollution from the smokestacks of pleasure mongrels. The glow of righteousness has been buried by the grave-digging spades of the wicked. The gleams of hope have been misdirected by the mirrors of the carnal devotees. The shimmering of truth has been twisted into knots of hypocrisy by the deft fingers of secular seditionists. The halo of brotherhood has been straightened into the spear of oppression by the forges of the media whores. The spotlight of God's Word has been painted over by the brushstrokes of the professors of mendacity. The nimbus of Christ is being slain by a hysteria induced, hate driven, duplicity orchestrated mob of supercilious disciples of the flesh.

Noose

Caught in the gallows of time we swirl in the mists of sedition. Held fast in the lariat of repetition we turn back to our vomit of transgressions. Trapped in the garrote of our failures we struggle vainly against love. Snared in the loop of trepidation we wrestle with our desire for equanimity. Lassoed with the rope of inclusion we become entangled in the red rose thorns of the hoi polloi. Gripped in the clutches of the vine of expansion we trample the wheat of the innocent. Hanged by the gibbet of choice we abandon wisdom for foolish pursuits of vanity. Haltered by the bridle of manipulation we give way to the hands of misdirection. Buckled to the steering wheel of the mendacious we are consumed in the crash of conformity. Looped in the coils of opulence we tread upon the torn cuffs of the impecunious. Twisted in the helix of ecumenicalism we veer from the auspices of truth. Lynched by the vigilantes of superciliousness we are cut off from the voices of reason. Slain by the nooses of the perverse, the virtuous cry out for expiation of justice.

Obituary

The final words at the cessation of earthly life give litany to the exploits of the celebrated. The last rights give rise to blossoms of insight. The memorial services tickle the faithless with tendrils of hope. The cenotaphs etched into the stones of timelessness give reminders of firm beliefs. The shrines of memory markers along the interstates of pain shed light upon the forgotten. The mausoleums of the well-preserved give crystal whispered hope of life eternal. The crypts of solidarity are sewn together with the threads of harmonious cherubim concertos. The tombs of the obedient reverberate with echoes of dedicated footfalls. The sepulchers of the saints resound with the testimonies of truth. The vaults of the martyrs cry out with the drops of blood of the faithful. The catacombs, of the forgiven, show the way through the maze of deception and point the way to the flowing waters of life.

Ordainment

Decreed by the action of the unwavering, truth is embedded in the stones of the virtuous. Proclaimed by the voice of reason, affirmations of faith are smelted into the manacles of Love. Announced by the shockwaves of the supersonic jet fighters of the blameless the battle for grace falls on the ears of the unfruitful. Established by the slain Word, our pardon is granted by intercession. Brazed in iron by the scribes of hope, our striving produces hidden abundances. Commanded by the voice of Creation, the firmament is established in the delicate silk strands of belief. Ordained by conviction, the bondsmen of morality row the boats of liberty through the murderous waters of the anti-Christ.

Our lives are our own

Our lives are our own, or are they? We navigate through time with a compass or GPS. Like butterflies on the breeze we flutter & flap randomly. Is this the sum of what we should be? Our roadmaps we draw. The life paths we pave. The destination we desire, we make. The purposes of our hearts we pursue. Like a bee after nectar, deliberate concentration. Anything less we determine is unacceptable. Could it be we strive with futility? Are our goals so shortsighted? With all our plans can we gain one year, one heartbeat? Whom do we slaughter on the way? Our father, our mother, children, friends are easy to expend. All around us are up to be offered. Everything that can aid us is consumed. Like feeding indiscriminately the flames of a fire we use everyone. Looking back we spy an abyss and a void of destruction. Arrogance, ignorance, pride, we see only what we want. We deem it enlightenment, success, accomplishment. What cost? Do we care? Free choice is ours but we can't see. With choice comes consequence. We have no clue the true cost. Our very being, self we gamble freely. The true path is not our own. Brother, sister, mother, father, friend God!   Our life path should be paved with the bricks of love!

Paint Cans 'n Puppies

Summer drew nigh and the year to paint the house was upon us.

Green trim and whitewashed walls were the plan, so I was told there'd be no fuss.

Green was my color as all could attest; a two year-old's artistic eye spied a green house.

Puppies that year were half dozen new, almost too small to run, scared of a tiny field mouse.

Not big enough to stand well, time was on my back being licked in the face more oft 'n not.

Six little pups run wild at will nipping and tugging Jet, Milly, Loopy, 'n Duke, Bell, 'n Spot.

The odd dog out Spot was the runt like me and into everything, trouble his middle name.

Spot a constant friend every step I made he was there, trouble sought, found, Spot I gave blame

Paint day at last arrived I bided my time watched and waited till all eyes were in front.

The small corner in the back I drug my pail of green a paintbrush in hand not easy for a runt.

Green on white I soon slathered on thick my artist's eyes agleam till my name I heard a yell.

The slit twixt ground and house wide enough for a quick roll beneath feet passed by oh well.

The coast was clear and out I popped my busy brush spread the glistening green of my will.

My name got louder and the sounds of feet came near again I roll beneath the floor sill.

The feet strolled by and again I started out but my name changed to Mom and back came feet.

Mom yelled louder then more feet came round a hand shot under and my butt a switch to meet.

My artistry came to an abrupt end then no green house with white trim for me this day.

Soon the sting of my butt gone Spot at my heels a green puppy might be grand who could say?

Preachers and Frogs

Preachers and frogs are pretty much the same they call and call oft times in the rain.

They send out the word to reel folk in, one for lost souls one for a lady friend, oft in vain.

Their voices carry far and loud, or soft and low, always beseechingly they plead.

With song they draw, compelling, tire treads crush, pulpits splinter, and they bleed.

Frogs and preachers call out in desperation, lights and wonders untold, fired passions they fan.

One down the aisle Bible thumping, the other in the moss is jumping to avoid the frying pan.

Preachers and frogs call unto the night, imploring, seeking trying to draw the lost and seeking.

Green skins glistening, brows dripping, ladies fanning, and little faces over pews peeking.

Voices lifted in song the tent flaps reverberate the sounds outward the croaks bellow in query.

Fire and brimstone to bring the souls in, thrums in the water are to call in a lady friend leery.

Little eyes widen hell's gate paints the tent red, strong legs leap as croak's courtship is given.

Wooing draws to an end suitors' sounds echo, preaching hits a pinnacle the night is riven

Little hands loosen round the frog's belly, preacher a deep breath taken pauses for effect.

Big green frog leaps free, down the aisle hops franticly, spies round bellied preacher and croaks most abject.

Purged

Life given freely is purged through blood. Hope held tightly is washed free of any faithlessness by the unchanging promise. The blade of justice is forged in the fires of tempering flame and is acceptable and usable as a sharp sword. Defender of life honed to split hairs between lies and truth relinquished control into the hands of the Omnipotent. Freedom from enslavement to narcissistic gluttony has purged the final death from the strong threads of life. Separated from hate an eye for clear sight knows to have no respect of persons for self-righteous judgments against humility.

Wrapped in the living Word of the Omniscient is to be purged of all inequity. Cleaned and acceptable we can now kneel at the springs of the river of life. Refined as the purist gold, purged of impurities untold hold ready the adopted awaiting the Word. Age wracked and alone or days only since birth we're held tightly in the arms purged from all harm. Accept now the offer and be purged, freed from the weight of all burden's great harm. Go shouting your importance from the roof tops abandon hope and give into the scourge. Languish in your joys for short lived they will be. Un-purged you live enslaved waiting your fate. Brimstone's last failure will burn throughout the eons filled with hate.

Quagmire

Mired in a cesspool of folly grown deep and sticky with the incessant defecation of the faithless, the voices of hope are stifled. Swaddled to the neck in the wax of inequity drizzled from the candles of the ignorant, we embrace wickedness and name it our right. Bound in the webs of deceit spewed forth from the bowels of the Machiavellian, we try to hide from truth.   Sunk into the trenches of inglorious battlefields of reason, we become conditioned to the mad ravings of the damned seeking companionship. Caught in the quicksand of enlightenment poured forth from the cobalt pails of the media, we are submerged in pronouncements of deliriously enchanted lies. Captured in the whirlpool of oceans' colliding waves of politicians, we are drowned in the confusion of power mongering fools. Lost in the inky depths of the caves carved in the basalt, we are prisoners of the wealthy. Restrained by the fruitless vines of the unwilling, truth becomes beaten to death by the whips of vocal malefactors. Cradled on the boughs of reprehensible denial, the forest fires of self-indulgent nefarious pimps blacken the innocent. Hung from the gallows of the degenerate, Love has been distorted into the propaganda of the iniquitous. The quagmire of final destruction is being stirred by the hands of all nations, and the price is an eternal brimstone bath. Repentance by multitudes will drill holes of grace in the stone lined bathhouses of sin scalloped fortresses, and drain the sewage that we have chosen to wallow in, giving opportunity for eternal life to sprout from the destruction.

Quicken

Life enters at the opportune time and the angels rejoice. At rest between the stars it awaits the Word spoken into the void. Chosen before the foundation of the universe was poured into the mold of hope the appointed time was given. Hastening out of the deep, the whales' songs boom with harmonious chords played to life's celebrated inauguration. Purpose soars on the wings of eagles' lofty watches waiting to be plunged into the bosoms of the birthed at the quickening. The footfalls of grace carry the weight of the children across the beaches of probation. The knees of arbitration strike the frozen ground of the stray's path and become bloodied. The elbows of mercy dig deep into the clay of selfishness and lift out the child of faith. The hands and feet of Love are pierced with the spikes of guilt and the penitent are emancipated.

Quietus

The final hour tolls from the Big Ben of life's clock tower. The account books are opened to the ledgers of life's endeavors. The review begins at the midnight hour of life's expedition. For some the scale is balanced with the weight of accepted grace and they are redeemed. For others the pendulum of judgment is tipped to one side with the load of innumerable slammed doors. The iron bars of retribution gape open into the gulf of perdition's eternal brimstone. The yammering of the guilty is quieted by the convicting voice of the Judge's review. The forever lost cry out with voices of recognition of their blood stained trousers of slain opportunities. Guilt can no longer be denied and the hands of opportunity can no longer be rewound. The soft knock of request to enter the heart has been stilled and will never tap again. The final tick of the second hand of grace has been immobilized by the stone grip of death. The redeemed shed tears of gratitude mixed with sorrow for the unrepentant. So few cling tightly to faith, hope and love to the quietus of the books of cleaned slate. The hoards of lost souls cling stubbornly in ignorance to the chains of refusal until the weight of their own choices can no longer be upheld and the final failure at the very end of life's race is irreversible.

Rainbows

Rainbows are God's promise given long ago; we best not forget the true symbol of life, of love. The times grow dark as they have many time before, the clouds of hate thicken and choke life lost. Warnings ignored, our own lives to live, our own terms to give, we desert our one Hope above. Discard enlightenment, plunged into shadows, believing we are first to delve and we ignore the cost. Rainbows and teardrops intermingled glisten as dew in spider web's myriads of light. Compassion and love are long lost in the bustle forgotten we pursue pleasures of no worth. Someone loves you beyond words, why then do you hate, free will builds our own plight? Is fantasy we're told faith without understanding the learned wrestle with the immaculate birth. What intelligent person slaughters one who loves them beyond life? Many, history is fact? If the one who loves won't conform to the will of the masses then death makes perfect sense. Better to slaughter the one who loves than to consider putting aside lusts, hate; we lack. The act was done to cover the failure of the Pharisees, teachers, law givers, in darkness hence. History repeated the masses again deny, ignore, hate condemn the One who loves beyond life. Why? Because they say he excludes those who disagree, who hate, who would destroy, rend. They proclaim enlightenment, know more than God and refuse to forgive, love not and work strife. Shout from the rooftops their sins to decree, deceits to seduce the naïve always to life's end. Rainbows God's gifts assuring no more mass cleansing with flood waters corruption's scour. At the last we become like the first seduced completely, revelry and debauchery forever we seek. Patience and long suffering, hope without hope delayed and the purging fires are withheld until the final hour. Perfect love slaughtered continually, our own knowledge we determine is best, many hearts reek.

Ransom

Hostages held in the darkest dungeons of our own design we diligently construct walls of stone egocentricity and are imprisoned. Hijacked by desires, hopes and carnal goals we turn the key to the lock of consciousness and are satiated. Abducted by opulence we count the gold coins of our destruction and rejoice in ignorance. Snatched into the breath of conformity we accept the lies of the deceived and wallow with them in the depravity of abominable acts. Seized in the claws of the snow crabs of impiety we deny our error and declare all are free to pursue immorality without consequence. Sequestered in the jury room of the nefarious we are subjugated to the influence of repetitious media blitzes and succumb to their conditioning acceptances. Incarcerated with inequity's embrace we resolutely cling to the thighs of peccadillo and drool on our own red drenched robes. The key of our freedom was nailed to a cross and a door to grace was erected. Our Liberator accepted our punishments and was raised to make intercession for all. Our deliverance was assured by blood and by separation and we all hear the knock of freedom. Our ransom was paid in full by the blood of the innocent and our redemption was founded in the corner stone of life. Alas, how many the multitudes that stand in the house of the kidnapped and ignore the knock of the Glorious Liberator because of hardened hearts of indifference.

Rift

Spades of choice delve deeply into the foundations of the bridge to eternal life and the way is cut off. Mallets of dissention tap incessantly at the granite of faithfulness and the traitorous fracture hope. Plows of division slice through the soil of unity and the seeds of malice are sown deeply. Rakes of confusion scour the landscapes of understanding until patterns of perplexity muddle the reasoning of the wise. Hatchets of hate chip away the bark of love until the sap of lies drowns the ignorant. The hammers of mayhem beat the iron horseshoes of resolve until they are bent into compliance with the mass will. The tongs of vengeance grasp the shackles of retribution and secure the bolts of attrition. The shears of clipped opportunity have severed the ropes of salvation. The scythes of the last harvest are poised to be thrust into the ripening stalks of wheat. The thresher of discernment will separate the chaff and it will be thrust into the fires of justice. The cleaver of the final judgment will open the rift of retribution and the unrepentant will shed their last veils of denial.

Sap

Life's blood flows at the first signs of spring. Hints of longer days entice, draw up into the light the tree's blood. Syrupy coagulations in the roots of time eon's memories preserved. History is recorded in the strands of gooey blood. Antifreeze imbedded in the flow of Hemlock's juices thawed through the winter it flows freely. Hickory, Oak, Ash slumber till spring life renewed with memories reawakened. Vibrations of Earth's groans ripple in evidence of God's voice, called into being. Songs whispered through slow chemical speech unheard by human ears' denial of the truth. Sap, Earth's blood flows into life at spring's heralding. Renewed for a time by the cycles of sunlight, rain, Earth's body devoured by photosynthesis. The juice of life is written in living word recorded through eyes that see, ears that hear and minds that are not closed. Time hints, truth rents, searched out and discovered by children's dreams among the flowers of leaves. Hidden in plain sight from eyes that cannot see God's melody fled from the grasp of the wicked. Songs of life are sung loudly in summer. Shouted joyous renditions of love are silent to the deaf ears of liars. Sap's vinyl record of God's creation song preserved since the foundation for ears that can hear. Children listen, hear, and rejoice in the celebration of life played by the sap's golden music. Unhindered, free as children we must be to perceive the sound of God's voice. A quiet walk among the trees in spring listening with a child's ear we may hear the truth. So hearken to Love, let go the lie, become like a child and learn the way.

Sassafras and Teaberry

Thirst is a tromp through the woods without a drop of water

Heat swelters down humid air tightening its grip as the kiln of a potter.

Up a dry holler and over the ridge I go not even a bead or drop on the moss.

Hog back ridge is bone dry as well nothing to slack my thirst remove this cross.

At every ancient spring I stop probe with questing fingers but no dampness I find.

I look up, the skies are clear no hint of thunderstorm the heavens aren't kind.

My trek stretches before my eyes the end not yet even in sight.

The day's frolic has become an unending search; sun's rays weigh down its hot

might.

I trudge along lips stuck like bald tires in thick mud.

My tongue is now useless no moisture does it impart, if there'd only been a flood.

Water would have been pooled to find every holler would have offer.

But alas no rain since July the parched ground groans for water from heaven's coffer.

Another mile behind me and finally a small respite I find, benefactor, but no drink.

A slender sassafras tree stands in my path quick snap young shoot lips open from a

brink.

The sweet tangy sap brings blessed saliva to a broil at least lips can be wetted.

With sharp cracks two more young limbs in my pocket I've netted.

Another ridge behind and a holler before, but no water I've found.

At least the north face is cooler a small gift of the mountain, where am I bound?

Oh, yea to Aunt Rebecca's for a fresh pie slice.

Just a few steps farther a boon again mountain teaberry leaves shine, how nice.

Shriek

Flung, torn and shredded from the paths of truth ripped and frayed as the edges of a paper ripped from the spiral bound notebook of life. Ignorance wanders lost among the confusion of lies and deceit. Challenged and deferred to the end of life responsibility has been murdered. A slow painful death at the hands of irresponsible pleasure seekers slaughtered by ever-growing lusts, truth has become ineffectual. Noah's bane reborn resurrected by the history challenged that are blind to all past mistakes, the blissfully happy follow the light of the fallen one into darkness. Damned by an ever spiraling weight of blame we place on the innocent to avoid self-incrimination. Objects are responsible people are not. Circumstance causes evil perpetrated by the puppet controlling the puppeteer. We dance on the stings of incompetent lies of conceit. Abandoned, the innocent are given over to those who would consume all that is good. Eaten by the ravenous wild hogs, responsibility has been defecated out into the muck of our fantasized enlightenment. We are fallen, have leapt, and are plunged willingly into the abyss of the joyous raptures of Hell. The hand of life is extended to all who stand at the very brink. Hate trodden, spit upon and ridiculed to death and beyond by the lies of the ignorant learned the Redeemer's abuse at the hands of the wicked continues. History is repeated in an ever-downward spiraling pattern. Wandering and alone by choice we slap the outstretched hand that holds eternal joys. Evaluate before the plunge take hold and clasp tight the truth. Recognize the King's crown of thorns, open the doorway to life and take firm hold of Love's outstretched hand and be rescued from the abyss of perpetual hate. Become snatched from the maw of eternal death and shriek with glorious joy instead of true terror's cry.

Smiling Tyrant

Smiling face, twinkling eye and mask of death go unrecognized and hidden bought by dreams of fire. Lies easily swallowed by eager hearts are sweet when words utter global epidemic desires. Appeals are for the poor, riches to spread, wealth abounds for all a gift offered without price. Hungry eyes seeking ever groping for something without effort or cost death's toll twice. Rome renewed, money paid and bought with honey promises of immortal contract made. Shadowy death stalks the gates of victory, waiting, the owed debt of first dirt is in the spade. The grave comes slow unrecognized it is an abyss of blackest depth hollowed by our own votes. Lewd money and soft words seduce the easily swayed and we follow willingly to our slaughter and are blindly deceived as he gloats. Destruction is of our own construct as coveting our neighbors' wealth we fall prey to the raptor of popularity. Soaring wings lifted by lusts of power, money is a hot fire we've elected our own captor. Worshiped, saluted, chosen by the majority self imposed slavery of greed ever we seek. Images of wealth for all, history is repeated, Hitler is reborn and enthroned anew and hidden in lies is death's reek. Our abyss grows as we pour efforts into immoral endeavors to the ease of debauchery dances a waltz to the melody of accusations. We care only for ourselves. Who can get us there more quickly as no debt is too great for our voracity? Enlightenment we claim to be as into the Dark Ages we plunge blindly delving backward 2000 years into the past. Concealed easily from those who choose not to see our 239th year may very well be our last. Quickly seek our hearts' desires through perversions seductions we delve into decadence. The lock to our prison freely clicked, chosen it is embraced into lusts of spreading precedence.

Snowflakes and Soot

The soft gentleness of the falling flakes quietly rustles.

The day's duty calls, slumbers depart, breakfast preparations bustles.

The cook stove is cold, the fire's embers slumber in the ashes.

The aged hands work in a few pieces of bark and kindl'n from lard pail stashes.

A gentle breath coaxes the lone ember softly the glows deepen.

A tendril of smoke, a bunny of soot rises and up the flue it goes a creep'n.

Patience of Job no match to waste the cracked lips persist.

A flicker, a spark of small blue-gold flame withers a tongue to insist.

A blazing fire is laid the oven glows hotter as snowflakes glitter on the window pane.

Hands move with eighty years' practice no thought given no waste or strain.

Chicken breaded, apples sliced, biscuit dough is kneaded.

Eggs lay ready, cast iron pan seated, lard on the stove is heated.

The day's light not yet broken there's no pale glow in the eastern skies.

Snow is now layered on the window like ice cream on pies.

Potatoes now pealed waiting their turn, chicken browning in hot oil spattering.

The chill is now driven out into the morn, teeth are still no longer chattering.

Oven is ready, biscuits formed, tops brushed with yesterday's bacon renderings.

Rising, browning, cracking, aroma is wafting floor to ceiling in its meanderings.

Smells abound in mouth watering scents overflowing, permeating every room.

Little beds rattling, little feet pattering on the plank floors scurrying for warmth soon.

Kitchen is now toasty the dining room too night shirts are trailing.

Little faces smiling from their eyes sleep departed little noses smelling.

Stubby fingers are reaching for samples, tastes, morsels snatched secretly.

Old eyes sparkle pretending not to have seen the gay pilfering allowed discreetly.

Soot and ash on the snows from the breakfast fires mingle.

The children stand laughing cold toes warming fingers alive now with a love tingle.

Sparrows

The chirp, chirp, chirp in the soft morning light heralds the new day's dawn. Numbered, known counted to the very least celebrated life's marvelous songs. The moss gives testimony of the night's passing. Bright green fronds sing the darkness's ending. Seeds and beetles feed the tiny mouths. All are counted, numbered and known. The tree's leaves in the early light whisper truth heard in nature's song. The hawk's cry, the dove's coo, in harmony with the whispered truth's acknowledgment of life, give proof to the abundance of love. Counted, treasured gifts to the poor, all are more valuable than golden hoards. Butterflies on the buttercups glowing in the sunlight are sparkling witnesses of the final hours. All numbered from the egg are named in intimate contentment of the times. The final hour counted in milliseconds of sand grains falling one at a time through the hourglass of the eons. The final day's dawn the brightest in ten thousand years gives the last light to the unknown dying. Celebrate the rebirth of death unto new life forsaking the lie given at the garden. Fruit and sparrows, trees and flowers, tall grass and sweet herbs essence waft truth among the stars. All numbers are known, counted as the stars, named fêted with the stripes of love. Birthed by love eons past through the gates of the forsaken delivery abandoned reason. At each sparrow's fall and at each star's naming the song of life is sung through time and space until the eon's ending.

Spider Web Cries

Come into my pleasures and hang here with me. Freedom awaits your first grasping hand. Step into my parlor and feel the sweet dreams. They are free for the taking just come and see. Pleasures untold you will find on my threads. Light here so softly and be bound in my bed. Joyous release I offer to thee. So reach out one finger and place it here beside me. On the hammock free of cares I'll rock you to a pleasant lullaby. Come into my parlor and see for yourself, freedom waits there for you, you'll see. Sweet words of praise and flattery go far. Enticement and temptation lead steps along a broad thread. Easy to step onto, hard to step off of beguiled by the easily swallowed lie. Charmed with a song of the most beautiful kind, alluring, inviting it leaves none behind. Falsehoods abound with what we want to hear. We hearken and hasten ignoring all fear. In truth we know they are lies but don't care. Search for all our desires leads to a snare. Hung by our feet in the webs of deceit, wrapped in threads we've woven too tight no escape can we find from the night. We are now stricken with venom of the senseless kind lulled into slumber thinking it most sublime. Fears are all sated and forgotten in dreams. Blissfully happy we hang caught in the darkest dream.   Right up to the stab of the deathly spike we dream our silly pleasures believing all unseeing. Liquefied in the end our life sucked slowly out Spider Web Cries release no sound but death's silent night.

Spring Time on Laurel Fork

The does stand guard with ever watchful eyes.

The fawns run kicking and jumping no danger do they spy.

Hawks shrill cry, cardinal's quiet plucking last year's berries everything anew.

Frost on the grass sparkling with sun's fire, a restful sound is the dove's morning coo.

Hesitant chirp, chirp sounds out the call of a half thawed cricket.

The morning mists swirl between the trees and the thicket.

The creek babbles softly along descending every more quickly.

The minnows dart ever watchful for a meal under the ice crystals so prickly.

The stillness broken by the jackhammer of a woodpecker's incessant pounding.

The thrum causes my heart to try to keep pace in my ears ever sounding.

A powder blue sky swirls by above me the sun to my right the moon to my left.

High cirrus clouds waft by like the mists among the thorns they most deft.

The cows are bawling and are ready to be milked they hurry lowing.

The pail rattles loudly hoping the milk not to be spilt as carefully we watch where we're going.

First walk through the frost dotted grass dappled with dew in the sunlight.

The crickets to the heather they return tired from songs sung all-night.

I trudge steadily on shoes soggy wet to my knees.

A few blooms through the frost peaking herald a few hardy bees.

Thoughts of honey and hot fresh biscuits bring my mouth to a smile.

Fresh cow pies by the gate, mud past my ankles the last steps like a mile.

The day's milk to bring home is a chore I am told.

But with fresh buttered biscuit and honey with milk I wash down, a great day to unfold.

To milk the cows is no chore especially in spring.

The bounty is plentiful the reward refreshing that a little work I bring.

A smile and a laugh are the greatest treasures.

Sunlight and springtime on Laurel Fork bring the most pleasures.

Starlight

The first twinkle at dusk is herald of diamonds strewn through a fiery universe
divine.

As the mists rise, the breath of earth exhaled on a cold winter's night a veil to beauty
unbound.

The glittering grows in ebony backdrop of the sky's stage falls fifteen billion years
of prime?

Fiery white, sterling silver tinkling soundlessly, eyes look up dreamily ransomed
expound.

Dark light slumbers in shadows waiting hunger gnawing the wind biding the proper
time.

Mutely death stalks the appointed to reap a gruesome harvest silent leaf falls no
sound.

He who is last comes first the frost given gift reflects diamonds in the grass
withered rhyme.

Time without record of the forgotten is lost, unbidden come forth to life's flaming
mound.

Gifts of hope journeys hinted offered not accepted free none the less unshackled
from crime.

Lights burn away the inky wraith of hate as cloth held to the flame holes of a bloody
crowned.

Starlight the gift of the night skies far beyond earthly treasures what do we value in
our wine?

Blazing hosts bear witness to truth unchanging once dipped in the blood we are
cleaned, found.

Diamonds more worth than gold we need just stretch out a hand to grasp a love most
sublime.

Flashing light from above reflected below colors all aglow beckon us out of the
ground.

Reborn dust to dust returned drawn up again from sleep, the tomb bathed the scent of thyme.

Choices to make starlight to consider accept wisely or deny foolishly the offer this time round?

Steer Fork Jig

The twang of a banjo and the hum of an old guitar blended harmonies sound.

Thump of boot and swish of dress twirl and stomp on the old barn floor round n round.

Arms' entwine and smiles boast of happy times and joy lets loose.

The caller's sharp bark instructions given, bodies dip and twirl tighten up the noose.

Knees rise high, hats are doffed at arms' length held, heads bowed with a hand to hip.

Ladies curtsey dress tails lifted from the dust held tightly, little fist steady the quick dip.

Music tightens, quickens with each beat the caller barks more urgently now the command.

The clap boards reverberate while music hugs the challenge goes out from Steer Fork Band.

The pulse quickens and feet hasten the pace picks up and movements flow.

Sweat drips from noses flaring, breath comes ragged now wait the end feet to reap and mow.

The crop of the dance culminates in a harvest's joyous song plant the first step garner the last.

The music ends, stings are silent, feet stop, faces glow, hands clap for that which's just past.

The Steer Fork Jig has rung its last, feet stroll to stools and tables at hand, dad leads mother.

Ladies go one way, gents the other, sweat drips from the brows of one, dabbed from the other.

Talk begins in murmurs, smiles plaster every face turned up, breaths to catch awhile to wait.

The band meanders, milling about a few hands carry flasks to lips a small nip thirsts to abate.

A quick break, breaths caught sweat barely dried the music begins again the first step seeded.

The caller rises, feet move forward responding to melodies explain the movements needed.

Expressions life force shown explained in the movement and words hard works culminate.

The months of labors are passed and the time of bounty has fallen time to celebrate, ruminate.

Stricken

The depths of our narcissism nail us to the walls of slavery.

Blinded by our own deceit we ignore advice from our closest friends' bravery.

Stricken without acknowledgement, blinded, our eyes no longer see.

Sought but not found we look in the wrong places ignoring God's plea.

Lost we refuse to be rescued, armed with denial, we defend against Love.

Wrapped in darkness, plunged into the abyss we refuse what's from above.

Impaled with ignorance the more knowledge we gain, utterly stricken.

The soup of our desires we boil through life our own quagmire we thicken.

Hate masked in tolerance but no forgiveness offered we damn those who are different.

Woven intricately into the fabric of our despair till enemies we become equivalent.

From freedom to slavery the broad path leads us along in a fevered race.

Narcissism binds us into faithless chains as forward we rush into its cold embrace.

Slain is love for any other as we fall quietly into the shark-toothed maw of midnight.

From the light we flee in a hurried rush as terror snatches us into its heinous flight.

To turn toward truth and the narrow path is the last choice before our final fall

We best make the choice soon and walk truth's road, God's answer to evil's call.

Sunshine and Blackstrap

The early fall sunbeams hold warmth enough to thaw the core.

The cane is gathered, the mule ready and the mill cleaned ready for the pour.

The fire is hot and the kettle is shined waiting the sap to render.

All hands gather round the ole' cane mill belly up to the tarnished fender.

Ole' Blue is now tethered to the turnstile and he knows his pace.

Each task allotted as all here know tis an all day race.

The first stalks in and Ole' Blue moves forward without a word spoken.

The light mist wafts by as the sunlight glistens new heat given as the day's token.

The sun creeps up as Ole' Blue plods round.

The green juice starts a drip, then a trickle and soon a half bucket maybe a pound.

The first sled full is emptied the second waits near ready to be fed.

Each knows his task carry, feed, pull, stir, skim it's a long time before bed.

The day's task has just begun Ole' Blue twitches an ear at the crew.

Laughter at jokes fills the air, songs lifted up nothing here to rue.

Dinner time comes but no break is given and no shade she finds.

Fried chicken leg in left hand work with the right but no one minds.

Afternoon drags and shoulders grow weary, arms ache and backs stoop.

Foam begins to roll in earnest now the skimmers make a merry troop.

The day's work nears its end and the final lap is now in sight.

Ole' Blue senses his task most complete his last laps become a flight.

Granny comes teetering with her flour-sack lined wheel barrow full of jars.

Gray head bobbing, jars a clanking, her old hands are strong but show many scars.

Table cloth spread is crisp with starch just to her liking.

Jars laid five rows deep the whole length; to fill them all takes much hiking.

Blackstrap jar filling is her chore.

You best not get in the way or your knuckles will be sore.

Taken

Taken before their time, so we believe them to be, lost for a season to those who mourn. Taken by the hand to the place of rest we cannot fathom the reason. Taken away in the prime of perceived life our hearts are left tattered. Taken from life as babes we weep in ignorance. Taken out of our arms to be cradled in pure love waiting we lament our loss. Taken out of time and place lost to our eyes unseeing we grieve without knowing. Taken from our clutches as we try to hold tight we weep for ourselves as we grasp for understanding. Taken are our candles of hope and we wander in darkness. Taken and torn in heart and mind we hold vigilance against the hopeless despair of the evil one. Taken with anger we rage against life's seeming unfairness. Taken with grieving over our own uselessness we struggle to breathe. Taken by anguish our heads slip quietly into the murky depths of despondency. Taken away half our soul was ripped asunder and left to be trampled under foot by the yapping hyenas of deceit. Taken by the hand of God for a purpose of good we can't see we question why. Taken our cries are hurled out and swallowed in the darkness between the stars. Taken our hearts ache with loss unimaginable. Taken in despair we may drown in whispers of the evil one. Taken back if we hold tight to the light of faith we are comforted. Taken into the shelter of love if we hold tight to our hope we are relieved. Taken home to be reunited once again if we accept the offer of love we are redeemed.

Thanksgiving

Breath, blood and heart's life forces like the flares from sol.

All gifts are from above without which we are nothing, dust.

Cell's designs of Love's life flow stamped made as if a doll.

Give thanks this day for life's a gift freely given, just.

Breathe for joy wrapped in happiness not our own found.

Sunlight and starlight shine upon all formed, conformed to His will.

Be thankful for all; remember from where we came a small dust mound.

Nothing more than a breath of life on the chaff from the Miller's mill.

Rain and sun on the day's crops growing new life is given freely.

Abundance is overflowing with milk and honey rich beyond measure.

In our mirror's image we praise, thank and worship our own labor weekly.

Why do we believe ourselves to be the source of all our treasure?

Too quickly we forget our own breaths are counted, numbers of health.

Allotted according to His plan, they are gifted openly to all.

Our thanks we withhold hoard as a miser his wealth.

To thank our true Benefactor divine seems beyond our grasp, we fall.

Fail, crumple, ruin, heartache and disease for all we ask why.

If hearts remain closed, eyes unseeing we face the doom of our construction.

Our eyes we must turn heavenward thanksgiving better be loosed, let go glad cry.

Give heartfelt thanksgiving every day to God above or face alone our destruction.

The Lost

Abandonment of reason is a response to fear, disjointed, random, and lost.

Those who desire power foster fear, terror, hate, and do not count or care the cost.

The People relinquish power when fears are fed with lies, they're subjugated, enslaved, lost.

The powerful revel in their iniquity, wallow in self proclaimed piousness, freedoms are tossed.

Democracy has been taken, stripped by fear and avarice, usurped by the powerful, lost.

The masses in ignorance led blindly to deaths by lies, fools of power insatiably glossed.

A free state is only free so long as the people rule, so lies are given to seduce the lost.

Hunger for power, control by the authorities, taken by lies, illusions, diamonds of frost.

Cold encased, bound in iron manacles, hands extended locking their own shackles, lost.

Big government binds the willing slaves to fear, controls, fat with power, it can't be crossed.

Money spent we do not have a chain around the albatross's neck weighted unto death, lost.

Tyranny runs rampant given over freely by the fearful governed by lies, societies exhaust.

The charge to government is to be austere, penny-wise rigorous principles, strictures not lost.

Peoples at time must shake loose seek enlightenment and truth take task the powerful to accost.

The wolves are in the sheep pen, ravenously thrashing about slashing those in ignorance lost.

Do the sheep smell the slaughter of truth, or do they listen to the media's lies blood embossed?

The oppressors exult in the gore of the fall, engorged for a time until in their own vomit lost.

The powerful have seduced and bound us all by their bloody revelry, freedom is sauced.

Truth's Freedom

Freedom is elusive at best temporal within reach but never caught.

Truth abounds for all to see, elusive for many their sight clouded by what they've been taught.

Aristotle, Pasteur, Edison, and Columbus what if they'd held to the science of their day?

What truth a flat earth, a leech for a doctor, candle for light, stars circle earth, say?

If we all follow science's teachings without question what would we have, what truth's price?

Truth stands to believe or deny, unchanged from the start unquestioned once, twice, thrice.

Freedom is here in truth to be found who has wisdom let him hear, she who love has let her see.

Truth is near hidden hands cover our ears, sight blinded by tears, no truth where will we be?

Truth's freedom is free for the taking it requires recognition and a willing embrace.

Where now those who can see lost in the herd, sheep mentality we flounder lose truth's race?

Freedom's true meaning is not easily discerned a clear eye, open heart, wise mind are required.

Where now those who seek, study, question the status quo, in the hustle and bustle mired?

Too busy to care, too much work to see, truth escapes all who through life's struggles, flees.

Freedom a God given right the Constitution speaks of it outright but we've lost it in the trees.

Blindly we see that before our feet, in front of our noses, in our hands, but not any truth.

Lost in freedom to struggle and work, riches and wealth hoard we never read Job or Ruth.

The truth must be sought studied and pursued daily or else we are seduced by the lie. Freedom is only in truth and love, not in the lies and promise of riches, now's the time to cry.

Undone

We are undone by acts of attrition against those who hold the faith. We are undone by failure to give aid to those who suffer. We are undone by bearing false witness against the innocent. We are undone by worshipping the gods of greed. We are undone by fornicating with the harlots of malice. We are undone by coveting the spoils of our neighbor's endeavors. We are undone by the labors of fruitless striving for mounds of tarnished treasure. We are undone by the pursuits of the craven images of deceit. We are undone by the use of the name of God for the cursing of our enemies. We are undone by the disobedience against the instruction of our parents. We are undone by the murder of hatred against those who oppose our will. We are undone by the theft of our children's inheritances. Our inequity is undone by the repentant opening the doors of faith. Our damnation is undone by grace through faith. Our blackened hearts are undone by the white washing of Jesus' blood. Our hate is undone by the pure love of forgiveness. Our guilt is undone by the acceptance of debts paid by the riven body of our Redeemer.

Urgency

The walk of life's journey nears the end of the path and weary feet stumble at the brink of the abyss as the harps play a derelict litany. Directives disregarded chew up the pavement of smooth transitions with a flute's sharp cries. Into the silent nights strong hands muffle the ears of the unwilling against the warning bells' loud clanging chimes. The correction rod of discipline beat at the layered dust of the stubborn whose crusted rugs are the result of wayward dancing to the piper's seductions. The Judge tarries for a season's season stretching opportunity for repentances to those who listen to angel choruses. Written in words of instruction the assembling of obedience is a matter of perseverance against the tantalizing cabaret of burlesque. The teachings of the wise brush the coat tails of the preoccupied with the tapping of the drums of hope. The heralds of the ending of the age stand on the rivers of strife and proclaim the truth with the sounding of trumpets. The urgency of the final call peels out in R.S.V.P. laced announcements of the celebration of Love's triumphant orchestra of eternal life offers.

Usurped

Pilfered quietly by the hands of deceit, an offer of awareness was made. Plucked by desire, the fruit of knowledge was consumed and life ceased. Pinched with the stones of guilt, eternity was terminated by jealousy. Embezzled by soft spoken words of the deceiver, faith fled screaming into the light. Purloined by fingers of delight, sin was clasped to the bosoms of the tempted and its cloying fragrance permeated the air. Filched from the purse of the righteous, sanctity was corrupted by the hands of the immoral. Pocketed by the greedy, abundance was diverted and the innocent were left to dearth. Taken without regard, the naïve were delivered into darkness. Lifted from the cradle of paradise, eyes were opened to the world of suffering. Robbed of fellowship, willful disobedience walked boldly into fig leaves and fell. Stolen by choice, the blameless became polluted and were purged. Raided by the unwitting, the pantry of life was emptied. Ransacked by the armies of odium, the city of peace was shattered. Ravaged by the lusts of the abhorrent, the virtuous opened the thighs of guilt and succumbed to evil desires. Wrecked by the derailment of the train of truth, lies proliferated chocking the vines of hope. Usurped from the hand of the Omniscient, knowledge became an unguided wrecking ball and destroyed the tower of love.

Veneer

A façade of piety veils the ravenous wolf's hungry eyed groping of innocence. A layer of cherry wood coats the scales of the serpent hiding the darkness from the light seekers. A pretense of virtue holds the hearts of the deceived in a grip of enthrallment. A show of prayers delights the prideful arms of pomp and circumstance. A guise of radiance shimmers over the black cloak of hate. A coating of makeup hides the sores of the unjust. A shroud of religion justifies the murderous intent of the corrupted. A pall of smoke conceals the consuming fires of the iniquitous' evil acts. A blanket of ash covers the rock piles of attrition. A mask of obedience disguises the deeds of the rebellious. A mantle of oak sits above the soot of waywardness. A sheet of ivory wraps the exploits of the foolish in layers of ignorance. The veneer of lies must be shed down to the bones and blood of a contrite heart before the door of salvation may be opened.

Vigil

Quietly waiting in the last midnight hour, expectantly the dawning is searched. Breath held in anticipation of the arrival the wakeful kneel in hope. Hands quiver as wicks are trimmed in preparation. Feet fly under the unprepared who become stricken in oil-less flight. Hope grows with the lateness of the hour. The reluctant Bridegroom tarries, the chosen numbers have not yet been filled. Eyes seek out each new sound; attentively ears strain to catch the footfalls. Fingers nervously cling to the light, hopeful of the return. Toes curl in expectation of the Faithfull's reward. Knees lock in solid resolve of those who look forward to the return of truth. Vigilant steps keep pace with truth and prevail. The watchful enter in while the inattentive fall away captured by lies. The celebration begins as the last stray is gathered. The seduced yammer for equality with those whose vigil withstood temptations. The meek are gathered under the wings of the Dove of Peace and prosper. The haughty forsake truth to pursue their hearts' desires. Love's patience has ended with the final count's tally. Judgment descends upon the multitudes of oblivious deniers and they are snared by their own refusals of the truth.

Vista

The burden of truth is easily born on shoulders which are carried by faith. The weight of hope is as light as a feather floating on the breezes of love. The yoke of contrition is freeing to those who snap it in place with their own hand. The trials of a hard life hone the blades of recognition of instruction from above. The Word of salvation is translated for the ears of the repentant. The songs of the cherubim are joyous music to the ears of the steadfast. The twinkle of light shines boldly on the paths of the grace acceptors. The chain of love links all the flock into the corral of heaven. The mountains of sorrow are easily flown over on the wings of forgiveness. The sunset of struggles dawns on the vista of reward. The panorama of paradise awaits those who hold firm until the end.

Where have all the Joys Gone?

Our days are filled with untold joys.

Sunshine, a warm wind blowing what more need young boys.

Slingshot and summertime are full of promise and never ending possibility.

Old stones groan speaking the ancient tunes of their probability.

The trees sway and murmur in voices not quite as old as the stone's.

Roots curled digging to a depth then back out drying up like bones.

Leaves from last fall lie under an overhang great burial ground.

Hands burrow first into the dirt then a crevasse, a nook treasures to be found.

Acorns and hickory nuts scooped up to hoard, pockets to fill.

A boy's day a battle a war are the pleasure today they fit the bill.

Running, climbing and a tree to scale a daily plan has no value at all.

A pirate's ship or a castle gate has no limit the old rock face and endless wall.

A woodland boy has no worry of injury, blood or even life lost.

The day's fun a boy trails and tracks to find at any cost.

The pursuit of untold joys was such a simple hunt.

Young boys knew the path to confront.

A tortoise, a bug, a frog on a vine are all worth many an hour of time.

A stick, a rock and a length of twine a boy could rival anything in Mother Goose's

Rhyme.

Life is a joy we need only remember how; go back to youth if we can only see.

Move beyond the days worries and get back to the simple things, be free.

The joys haven't gone they are here to take.

Choose life, be true and make haste before it's too late.

Where have all the joys gone, we have posed?

Nowhere, I say it's we who fled many doors we've closed.

Where has all the fun been spent?

In our youth we explain as in our day we grumble but don't repent.

Our untold joys wait round every corner and unopened door.

We need only see, grasp and take opportunities offered and nothing more.

Whittled

Carved into the heartwood of hope, the repentant are fashioned into useful witnesses. Pared into the grains of faith, the stalwart are etched into figures of truth. Inscribed into the knots of love, the sinful are transformed into figures of purity. Cut into the limbs of intercession, the reprobate are pardoned into freedom. Shaped with the drawing knife of transformation the errant are converted into righteousness. Etched into the oak of life, the aberrant have been grafted into the tree of the forgiven. Notched into the block of discipleship, the chosen are tasked with witnessing. Trimmed into the vine of fruitfulness, the heirs sow seeds of the good news. Shaved into the likeness of purity, the transgressors postulate the robes of the children. Whittled with the tools of instruction, the humble learn to impart declarations of grace before the fortresses of ignorance.

Wood Ash and Lye Soap

The sun was always bright the air always warm the pot crouched over the embers of
the fire.

Wood ash was gathered, sifted finer than the finest flour, renderings made ready on
the pyre.

Granny's secret ingredients were laid by in a paper sack hidden from any prying eye.

First one then another added, stirred, bubbling, and steaming like the filling of a
lemon pie.

The smells grew wafting upward with the steam ever thickening with each stir.

Wood ash and sitch ingredients at hand anything and everything made to stand, its
soap sir.

The traveling salesman stopped by old mule at the gate his nose twitched a hot meal
to be ete.

He'd spied the big pot by the smokehouse steaming and thought a good meal he'd
get.

Rose petals wood ash and Lilac his nose finally discerned as I answered him again,
soap.

His disappointment was grand, frown complete he muttered an obscenity and turned
the dope.

If he'd only stuck round a moment you see, granny never turned a hungry soul from
the door.

Plenty he'd been given 'n even more hot coffee 'n a filled paper sack for his empty
belly sore.

But alas he weren't patient saw no quick sale here a poor widow's hovel he assessed
no more.

He mounted an ole mule doft he's fancy hat eyed my bare feet 'n said leave here son
ye'r poor.

I eyed him a doubt'n as the ole mule took out 'n granddad round the corner doc's bag
in hand.

I took the ole grey mare as granddad stepped down who wuz that he asked eye
roving the land.
Some quack salesmen didn't like granny's soap I reply in a grin as I led away ole
Beck.
Back to table the men piled in, food was hep'd high 'n overflowed waited my turn by
heck.

Xenolith

A ruby among the brimstones shining brightly out of inky despair, the Xenolith of hope shines a light of guidance. A diamond isolated in the coal seam of hate, the Xenolith of love binds the receptive. A gold nugget buried in the mountainous refuse of lewdness, the Xenolith of purity beckons the innocent. A sapphire flung into the quarry of inequity, the Xenolith of justice balances the scales for the forgiven. A pearl cast into the swine sty of the nefarious, the Xenolith of righteousness consumes the guilt of the grace seekers. A topaz trodden into the hard packed clay of the road to perdition, the Xenolith of warning utters dire cautions of an impending precipice to the abyss. A silver thread in the tapestry of the cast stones of condemnation, the Xenolith of forgiveness opens the eyes of the accusers. An emerald embedded in the quagmire of transgression, the Xenolith of obedience pardons the repentant. An amethyst bulldozed into the landfill of squandered opportunity, the Xenolith of resurrection gives new life to the faithful. An opal spiked into the cross of guilty pebbles, the Xenolith of paid debts removes the consequences of sin. A bloodstone fallen into the debris of Calvary, the Xenolith of intercession stands defending His sheep against the testimonies of the malicious soul prospector.

Xenophobe

The foreigner selflessness tugs at the heart strings of the empathetic and they reach out with kindness to aid the forlorn. The angst of the fallen gropes beseechingly through the catacombs of incipient deceit fleeing the fear with which it reeks. The trepidation of the spirit binds the hands of the ignorant preventing escapes into truth. The alien altruism sneaks past the walls of pride and bends the backs of VIP's until their foreheads touch the entangled humbleness hidden within. The torment of the wicked fractures the crust of hate and tendrils of zeal rise from the fires of perdition. The sorrows of self inflicted wrongs shed tears of faithlessness into the handkerchiefs of cupidity. The stranger gallantry rescues the damsel of despair and whisks her away on the white horse of hope. The phobia of compassion suffocates the breath of sustenance obstructing the trachea of encouragement. The terror of fearlessness sweeps the legs from under the hero of instruction and the explanations of faith are never uttered. The unfamiliar devotion to morality melts through the prison bars of depravity and unfolds the wings of freedom to be lifted on the zephyr of grace. The doubt of the timid keeps the weak of spirit from bursting forth from their paper house comfort zones. The skepticism of the deceived weaves a burial shroud of lies around their corneas blinding them to the manipulations of the wicked. The outsider to love can be salvaged from the junkyard of abhorrence by the electromagnet of Jesus' shed blood and xenophobia is conquered.

Xylem

My sap drips mingling with drops of blood from the hands of the Innocent. My heartwood beats in anguish to the injustice of a death undeserved. My leaves have fallen as the tears of the mourning are shed. My limbs quake in the tempest of shouts from the wicked. My bark is become stained with the crimson payment for the lost. My roots are set in the stones of the tomb readied gallows. My pith has been pierced by the spikes of hate. My foliage of life has been stripped by the hands of the ignorant. My branches have been dispersed offered unto the whole earth. My core has been riven by fiendish lusts of arrogant power-mongers. My veins have been stripped by the shards of lies flung in the words of hypocrisy. My xylem has been ruptured by those who fear Love.

Yearning

Thirst for truth has succumbed to the vortex of the drain of the deceived. Hunger for life has been devoured by the wolves of the ravenous hoards of acceptance. The ache for love has been massaged away by the fingers of the sexually immoral. The desire for hope has been sated by the pandering to debauched demands of purity. The yen for redemption has been nailed to the tree of fruitless indulgences. The longing for faith has been perverted into self reliant fabrications of the damned. The zeal for righteousness has been redirected into acts of hate mongering murderers. The fervor to carry the gospel to the ignorant has been burned away by the Pharisees of greed. The enthusiasm for succor has been stabbed by the swords of pride. The passion for forgiveness has been skewered by the spikes of the offended. The eagerness for inclusion has been extended by the hands of the nefarious. The craving for Christ has been smothered by the masks of the addiction cartels. The yearning for God has been robbed from the ignorant by the lies of science. Sought we refuse to be found, courted we refuse to be wooed, offered grace we refuse to be redeemed, given death we refuse to accept life, all in our yearning for a lie.

Yet

The guilty's trial is scheduled, yet their pardon they refuse. The indictment has been returned, yet the culpable ignore intercession. The accusations are verified by eye witnesses, yet the liable deny the truth of their guilt. The charges are innumerable, yet the blame is not accepted. The incriminations weigh heavy on the shoulders of the blameworthy, yet they point fingers at the innocent. The allegations are proved, yet the hypocrite declares his innocence. The offenses are without defense, yet the sinner rationalizes his actions. The crimes are horrific, yet the murderer declares they are justified. The transgressions are willful, yet the adulterer clings to his seductions. The indulgences were without ending, yet the greedy vow they have consumed only their fair share. The felonies are multiplied, yet the lawbreakers perjure their testimony. Their sins are overwhelming, yet the unrepentant spit in the shed blood of Love.

Yoke

The yoke of love binds the necks of the oxen of submission into the reins of freedom. The yoke of fellowship binds the strength of the steadfast into the harness of the Purveyor of truth. The yoke of hope binds the weakness of faith into the gears of unchanging guidance. The yoke of forgiveness binds the sinful into the doubletree of pardon. The yoke of discipleship binds the witnesses of truth into the collar pad of the testimonies of the gospel. The yoke of morality binds the repentant into the belly straps of the righteous. The yoke of resurrection binds the door openers into the halter of the flock of the Redeemer. The yoke of arbitration binds the bridles of the guilty to the hands of the Arbitrator. The yoke of accepted sacrifice splices the debtors into the chain of the Debt-payer. The yoke of eternity opens wide to accept the defendants holding tightly to the hands of their Liberator. The yoke of God must be lifted by the hands of willingness and clamped about their necks in obedience and humbleness before the enslaved are freed.

Zealot

Advocate of change for fear of truth and the scrambled pursuit of lies abound among the ignorant, multiplying the foundation's stepping stones to corruption. As sheep to the slaughter terror propaganda vending machines nail fear through the hearts of the unwise, sending them headlong into the paddock of the oppressors. Manipulation of the masses by misdirection through immoral smoke and mirrors has become the tools of tyranny. Fanaticism runs rampant weaving patterns of deceit between the fleeing legs of the lost herded through the fog of their controlled lives in full flight from themselves and truth. Addicted to fear and anger by the subtle hints of Hitler whispers shouted subliminally through media bombed minds, the luscious fruits of terrorism ripen. Defenses are gradually raped from the loins of the duped mistresses of politicians on their gold made beds of destruction. Truth has become warped by exploitation of the simple minded herd seeking shelter in the pastures of the carnivores. Terrorism has become domesticated by the would-be tyrants led to the abyss of carnage by sanctimonious nose rings of self-indulgence. Panic is on the verge of breaking out of the mold of history to flee headlong in to the repetitious mistakes of the woodpecker drilling incessantly into the same hole of emptiness. The final wall of correction will give way to the collapse of truth and the seekers will find themselves bound between the iron pillars of cruel oppression of their own creation. Hitler's ghost stands raving hysterically at the melt-down of the Chernobyl-istic world power-house that crumbled his would be empire into concrete wall fragments of repeated mistakes. Embraced by the decades conditioned puppets the zealot leaders prevailed and destructions burst forth from the ripened fruits of domestic treason sowers through subversive misdirection of the unknowingly enslaved. Changed, chained, the constitution becomes ineffectual shredded paper fragments of hopelessness and used to wipe the feces of hidden shame.

Zeitgeist

The epoch of Noah is again budding under the cultivation of the immoral. The era of the detestable has sprouted under the hands of the reprehensible. The age of malice has been fertilized by the lies of rationalization sown by the fingers of the deceitful. The time of fiends has been nurtured under the care of the wicked chopping down the vines of the hopeful. The phase of cruelty has been reared to maturity by the defamation of Christianity. The chapter of spite has been watered by the sprinklers of the vile to choke out the grains of the faithful. The period of abhorrence has been pruned by the sheers of indulgence snipping off the tendrils of worshipers. The interval of odium has been expanded into the fields of delight by the strokes of the scythes of the despair laden. The intermission of corruption has been spread onto the farms of the assiduous to propagate the idle handed. The moment of truth has been plowed under by the oxen of perjury and the ignorant have been duped. The occasion for nefariousness has been unfurled from the roots of reprehension and once again embraced after the flood of justice. The eon of sinfulness has been rotated from plot to plot avoiding the righteous fires of retribution. The generation of Cain salvages the spores of dissention to disseminate hate against the reverential in repetitious murders. The zeitgeist of Pontius Pilot has returned on the winds of infertility smothering the seeds of love under a blanket of blasphemous hatred.

Zest

Enthusiasm for truth has grown weak strangled by the brambles of lies. Gusto for love has been stamped out by the feet of the narcissist. Keenness for right has been bludgeoned by the clubs of apathy. Appetite for honesty has been devoured by the rending teeth of the prideful. Relish for virtue has been ravaged by the groping spears of the sexually immoral. Passion for blamelessness has been scorched by the flame of the deceitful. Fervor for good deeds has been cloven by the axe of egotism. Eagerness for pursuit of hope has been trapped by the furrier of despite. Savor of integrity has been left to die in the wilderness of dishonesty. Delight for the embrace of the arms of forgiveness has been pried apart by the wrecking bar of blame. Esteem for redemption has been withered by the heat of the desert of false prophets. Admiration for faithfulness has been bound up in the iron manacles of capriciousness. Ardor for grace has been riddled by the arrows of good deeds pushers. Zeal for acceptance of the free offer of mercy has been nailed to the cross of the unrepentant. Devotion for following the footsteps of Christianity has been martyred by the murderous pens of the law interpreters. Wholehearted acceptance of God's admonition has become mired in the quicksand of our nation's pandering with the gods of self-gratification. Zest for truth, hope, love, faith, grace, and pursuit of righteousness best be sought and grasped as tightly as a miser's coin to our national bosom before our final hour is declared and all choices are removed from the table of our enlightened Russian-roulette cylinder of sin.

Afterword

The truth may be whispered, shouted, proclaimed or denied vehemently, but in all cases it remains the truth. Whether you may have seen some hint of forewarning in these words, or may just have found them naively amusing is totally dependent upon your perspective and your willingness or unwillingness to look beyond your chosen façade of ignorance.

The bell of a lighthouse beckons with tendrils of warning into the foggiest, blackest night. An attentive ship's captain hears and responds wisely to avoid the granite teeth of the maw of destruction that awaits his charge. A bolshie captain ignores the truth, and navigates his charge directly into the ravenous gullet of cloaked destruction in order to carry out his desires. The first eventually sails out of the dark mists and into a glorious bright homecoming. The second in arrogance ignores the truth and eventually is swallowed by the maw of darkness from which there is no return.

Three thousand years ago the earth was flat and the sun revolved around it. These lies were accepted as fact without question by the masses because respected learned pillars of the community told them it was so. What lies do you cling to, without even a thought of searching for the truth on your own, because some self-proclaimed scholar has convinced you that his/her theory is fact?

A cautious gazelle hangs back from the forward rushing herd as they see an illusion of the feast. The herd pushes forward in a mad rush and either falls into the abyss or is consumed between the teeth of the cheetahs. The cautious gazelle looks for the truth hidden behind the seductions and veers away to avoid the horrid fate of the deceived.

These fragments of warnings are dappled with rays of brightness in order to contrast the two possible choices to be made. If we forget the simple gifts that bring great joy, then we have no thought of reward for turning from our selfish pursuits.

I implore you to think independently. For your own sake, study all things thoroughly until you can shred the cloak of lies and unveil the truth. In the end truth will remain, whereas lies will be exposed to the light and be burned away and the smoke thereof will rise incessantly.

CPSIA information can be obtained at www.ICGtesting.com
Printed in the USA
LVOW06*0815150813

348027LV00002B/2/P